Generating the Deity

Generating the Deity

Venerable Gyatrul Rinpoche

Translation by
Sangye Khandro

Snow Lion Publications
Ithaca, New York

Snow Lion Publications
P.O. Box 6483
Ithaca, New York 14851 USA
607-273-8519

Printed in the United States of America

ISBN 1-55939-055-7

Library of Congress Cataloging-in-Publication Data

Gyatrul, Rinpoche, 1924-
    Generating the deity / Gyatrul Rinpoche ; translation by Sangye
Khandro.
        p. cm.
    ISBN 1-55939-055-7
    1. Rdzogs-chen (Rñiṅ-ma-pa) 2. Meditation--Rñiṅ-ma-pa (Sect)
I. Khandro, Sangye. II. Title.
BQ7662.4.G93 1995
294.3'442--dc20   95-31326
                                                                                CIP

Contents

List of Plates

Ven. Gyatrul Rinpoche
Photograph by Robert Mizono

A Brief Biography of Gyatrul Rinpoche

The Venerable Gyatrul Rinpoche was born in the year of the Wood Ox, 1923, in Sichuan Province, China. Born into a noble family, he spent a happy childhood with parents and family members for his first eight years. In his eighth year Rinpoche was formally discovered as the reincarnation of Gyatrul Rinpoche, taken to Dhomang Monastery (an important branch of Palyul Monastery), enthroned and placed under the strict care of his root guru Tulku Natsog Rangdrol and other tutors. Gyatrul Rinpoche was formally discovered by Dzongzar Khentsey Rinpoche, who issued a statement detailing the young tulku's whereabouts, name of parents, place of birth and further particulars. This information was identical to the statement issued by Tulku Natsog Rangdrol.

Once enthroned at Dhomang Monastery, Rinpoche began many years of formal study and training. As a young man he maintained constant company with his root guru Tulku Natsog, spending many years with him in solitary retreat, moving from one isolated location to another. Rinpoche has studied under some of the greatest Nyingmapa mahasiddhas of this century and carries with him all the blessings and knowledge that he received directly from his teachers. Due to the onset of the Chinese invasion of Tibet, Rinpoche was told to flee his homeland, and his principal teachers even foretold the details of his future work propagating the Dharma in foreign lands.

Tulku Natsog Rangdrol, who was one of the five emanations of Dudjom Rinpoche (that of "concerned activity"), stayed behind, explaining that it was his karma to remain. After one year of tremendous hardship on the road to freedom, Rinpoche, who originally departed with a crowd of 20,000, crossed over the Nepalese border to safety with only 200 survivors.

In the years that followed he worked in the service of H.H. the Dalai Lama as well as H.H. the Karmapa. Later, in 1972, H.H. the Dalai Lama and H.H. Dudjom Rinpoche chose Rinpoche as the Nyingmapa representative to accompany the first group of Tibetans to be sent to resettle in Canada. After arriving in the West, Rinpoche travelled extensively around the U.S.A. and Canada at the invitation of Tibetan and Western disciples alike. In 1976 Rinpoche was asked by H.H. Dudjom Rinpoche, during His Holiness' second visit to the West, to be his spiritual representative. Rinpoche accepted this position out of devotion and, since that time, has maintained his loyal devotion to H.H. Dudjom Rinpoche by establishing many Yeshe Nyingpo centers in the U.S., including a beautiful retreat center in the Siskiyou mountain range near the border of California and Oregon. The site was consecrated by H.H. Dudjom Rinpoche and has hosted many great lamas as well as two wangchens (major lineage empowerments) given by H.H. Penor Rinpoche. The retreat center presently consists of 65 acres of isolated forest land and a four-story traditional temple. The temple is also the site of Rinpoche's residence when he is in the U.S.A. Since 1984 Rinpoche has been making regular visits to the Republic of China, Taiwan, where he has hundreds of devoted disciples. His skillful ability to explain the Vajrayana path in simple terms and his unfailing humor and compassion are the noble qualities for which he is most loved.

Preface

This commentary on the generation stage, presented by the Venerable Gyatrul Rinpoche, is based on the well-known root text written by the famous Tulku of Kathog, Tsewang Chogdrub. The root text is entitled *Kyed Pa'i Rim Pa Chog Dang Jar Wai Sal Ched Zung Jug Nyema She Chawa (bsKyed pa'i rim pa cho ga dang sbyar ba'i gsal byed zung 'jug nyi ma zhes bya wa)*, *An Explanation of the Generation Stage in Conjunction with Sadhana Practice called A Stalk of Non-dual Clarity*. Tulku Tsewang Chogdrub was a great scholar and became famous for his comprehensive explanations of the generation stage according to the Nyingma tradition. The root text is extremely concise, yet it includes all the essential information a disciple needs to proceed on the generation stage of practice.

The stages of generation are explained according to an understanding of the foundation of the purification, the cause for the purification, the purification and the result. In accordance with the view of the Great Perfection atiyoga, the foundation and result of the purification are inherently equal and identical. The cause and the process of purification are the basis for engaging in the generation stage practice, yet simultaneously one must constantly ascertain the view of the nature of the foundation and result while performing the practice stage. Each step in the practice corresponds to a step or stage in our development as a sentient being in cyclic existence. Since each stage in our ordinary development is due to a cause, the generation stage practice systematically purifies that cause, transforming it into the result which is none other than the originally pure foundation. By paying close attention to this procedure, maximum benefit and understanding will be derived from this teaching.

The Ven. Gyatrul Rinpoche has been teaching Vajrayana Buddhism in the U.S.A. since 1974. Originally sent to the West by H.H. the Dalai Lama and H.H. Dudjom Rinpoche, Gyatrul Rinpoche was appointed spiritual representative of H.H. Dudjom Rinpoche's Dharma centers on the west coast in 1976. Since that time he has assisted many Tibetan lamas in getting established in the West and has touched the hearts of thousands of Westerners from all walks of life.

As his translator, I have had the good fortune to work closely with and study under Rinpoche constantly since 1976. On many occasions Rinpoche has given excellent explanations of the meaning of the generation stage. He has often explained that it is essential for a Vajrayana practitioner to have an accurate intellectual understanding as a prerequisite for the profound teachings and practices employed in the generation stage practice.

Due to the request of many sincere disciples over the years, this teaching was given near Ashland, Oregon where Yeshe Nyingpo's retreat center, called Tashi Chöling, is located twenty miles to the south. Although the subject of the generation stage has been taught by Rinpoche a number of times, on this particular occasion a more extensive explanation was given. This is intended for serious, committed students who have developed a keen interest in this subject. The reasoning behind deity visualization and mantra recitation is so profound that indeed the curious seeker will also benefit greatly from reading this material. It is my sincere wish that this book may be of benefit to many fellow English-reading Buddhists who are engaged on this astonishing path.

I wish to thank Charles and Tara Carreon, who worked very hard to transcribe the audio tapes, edit the translation and arrange the table of contents, as well as Ian Villarreal and Kay Henry for their editorial assistance. In addition, I wish to thank Professor A. W. Barber, who has kindly assisted in the publication of this book. It has been a pleasure to reunite with Dr. Barber, an old friend and student of Rinpoche's, who is presently here in Taipei working and teaching. Due to his strong enthusiasm for this important subject, the opportunity to publish the book arose very naturally.

Finally, I pray that this merit may be distributed to all parent beings so they may one day be free from this round of cyclic existence. May this merit help to bring the swift rebirth of H.H. Dudjom Rinpoche into the world as well as the swift rebirth of Dzongnang Rinpoche Jampal Lodroe. May the lives of all great spiritual teachers be long and may good fortune and happiness prevail.

Sangye Khandro, Translator
Taipei, Taiwan
April 1989

Note to the Second Edition

With the reprint of this important manual, the prayers for the swift rebirth of H.H. Dudjom Rinpoche and Dzongnang Rinpoche have both been answered. May the lives of both of them and all great Dharma teachers be long and full of enlightened activity, bringing waves of benefit to all living beings.

Sangye Khandro
Ashland, Oregon
August 1995

CHAPTER I

General Introduction

To begin with, it is important to know that when you receive Dharma teachings, three types of motivation are possible. You might have a virtuous, positive intention, a negative intention, or a neutral intention that is neither positive nor negative, but merely dull and thoughtless.

You must eliminate negative and neutral intentions, which is done by recognizing them. You cannot do away with negativity until you recognize it, can you? Any kind of worldly intention is negative. All worldly intentions, such as hearing the teachings to obtain non-spiritual benefits, are considered negative. However negativities are expressed—through body, speech or mind—they should be eliminated.

All negativities are supported by the ten non-virtues. Of these ten non-virtues three relate to the body, four to speech, and three to the mind. The three that relate to the body are killing, stealing and adultery. The four corresponding to speech are lying, harsh speech, slander and gossip (idle words). The three of the mind are craving, ill will and incorrect view. If you don't know how these non-virtues are accrued, you should study the teachings on cause and result.

A neutral intention is a state of dullness or lack of awareness which is devoid of positive intention. This is not necessarily a negative state, however. You just attend the teachings in a stupid state, following the way a dog follows its master, or perhaps the way that a small child follows its mother. With this attitude, you don't really get anything out of what you are pursuing because you have no real intention or motivating force to begin with. Cultivating a positive motivation is a basic requirement to receive the teachings purely.

According to the Mahayana tradition of Buddhism, which is known as the greater spiritual pursuit, a positive motivation is the twofold intention to benefit oneself and others. This can also be expressed as having a single intention to cultivate the ten virtues, to perform all other virtuous deeds, and to achieve enlightenment, the level of ultimate realization, for the sake of benefiting oneself and others.

We call ourselves Mahayanists or practitioners of Mahayana Buddhism. Beyond that, we call ourselves *dzogchen* practitioners, or practitioners of atiyoga. Whatever we claim to be, whether Hinayanist, Mahayanist or dzogchen atiyoga practitioners, the main thing to remember is to develop and maintain the intention to hear and practice the teachings for the sake of oneself and all other beings.

Ngöndro, the preliminary practices that many of you perform on a daily basis, should not be thought of as mere "preliminaries." These practices begin with the Four Thoughts that Turn the Mind towards the spiritual path. These contemplations embody the essence of the Hinayana tradition of Buddhism, which is known as the lesser spiritual pursuit. The practices of *refuge, bodhicitta, Vajrasattva,* and *mandala* relate to Mahayana Buddhism, the greater pursuit, and the guruyoga practice relates to Vajrayana. All nine vehicles of Buddhism can be reduced to these three yanas, which are all practiced within the ngöndro. The ngöndro is a very profound practice that activates all three vehicles simultaneously. Because the three vehicles are all related, perhaps you can see the importance of contemplating the Four Thoughts and of cultivating compassion before you engage in Vajrayana techniques.

When Shakyamuni Buddha first gave teachings in this world of *samsara*, the very first thing he explained was that cyclic existence is a place of natural suffering. The realm of cyclic existence is by nature a place of suffering, turmoil and delusion. It is therefore essential that, before hearing the teachings and beginning any practice, you contemplate the Four Thoughts that Turn the Mind. Just as the Buddha chose to present these teachings before any others, similarly this is the first step in your own study of Dharma.

After considering the truth of suffering, proceed to cultivate an awareness that all other living creatures in the realms of samsara are in a state of delusion, just like yourself. All living creatures have, over the course of countless past lifetimes, been your own kind and loving parents, changing roles like players in a drama. All of these beings have brought you into the world at some time or another, and all of them, without exception, desire happiness and fulfillment. No one in this world of desire lacks the impulse toward happiness. They desire happiness; yet all the while, they create the causes for more suffering. What they desire and their actions of body, speech and mind are in direct opposition, but this irony remains unnoticed. In this way, like blind people, beings in samsara remain in bewilderment.

Now you are people who could be said to have vision and understanding. Further, your sense fields are fully endowed; you are not blind, deaf or mute. You possess and can realize the potential of a very valuable situation. You are able to realize and seize the opportunity to improve your condition. To make the best use of this favorable situation, you must contemplate the truth of suffering, cultivate compassion and engage in Dharma practices.

This teaching is about *kye rim*, "generation stage" tantric techniques. "Tantra" refers to Vajrayana Buddhism. There are two levels of tantric practice: outer and inner. These teachings are the inner level of tantric practice. It is very important to know the differences between these two levels. Some information is necessary before delving into this material; therefore, we will consider these two levels of tantric practices in brief detail.

The three outer tantras are *kriya*, *upa* (*carya*) and *yoga* tantra. The inner tantras begin with the *mahayoga*. There are major differences in the outer and inner tantras concerning view, practice, conduct, results and even the times during which a person practices. All of the tantras are in agreement, however, regarding initiation or empowerment: no tantric practice is to be done until the disciple has received initiation. Vajrayana can never be practiced without the perfect empowerment from a qualified master who holds the tradition of the lineage. This applies equally to kriya, upa (carya), yoga and mahayoga tantra. In both the outer and inner tantras four empowerments are given at the time of initiation. These four empowerments make it possible to practice the tantras.

The outer tantras are said to be difficult because results and realizations are achieved only through arduous perseverance. The inner tantras are said to be less difficult because results may be achieved in a much shorter time period, implying less difficulty. Further, the outer tantras require practitioners to perform many particularized activities, while the inner tantras, relatively speaking, are less concerned with contrived activities.

The outer tantras contain both kye rim and *dzog rim*—generation and completion stage practices. They are performed separately, and the generation stage is a prerequisite to the completion stage. This separation of kye rim and dzog rim is found only in outer tantra. The inner tantras combine kye rim, the generation stage involving characteristics and activities, with dzog rim, the completion stage which is void of symbolism, elaboration and activities. They are indivisibly joined and performed simultaneously.

The outer and inner tantras also take different approaches to personal conduct. Outer tantra practitioners maintain scrupulous personal cleanliness and purity of appearance, cleaning themselves several times a day and keeping a very clean external appearance. Inner tantra practitioners experience everything equally. This does not mean that they are dirty or crazy, but that they realize the equal nature in each situation without needing to constantly distinguish between good and bad.

Outer tantra practitioners are vegetarians, eating only the three white and the three sweet substances. They drink from beautiful cups studded with precious gems. Inner tantra practitioners may wear animal skins for clothing, such as human, tiger and elephant. Kriya tantra practitioners bathe in a ritual fashion three times a day and also put on clean clothes three times a day. This kind of conduct is prescribed for all three outer tantras. True inner tantra practitioners may never change their clothes. From the external point of view, such a practitioner may appear as a beggar or peasant.

In addition, there are big differences in the levels of realization achieved in the outer and inner tantras. Relatively speaking, it takes a long time to obtain results from practicing the outer tantras. In general, it takes sixteen lifetimes for a kriya yogi to achieve enlightenment, and on the path of yoga tantra it takes three successive lifetimes. To achieve enlightenment within these time frames one must practice very, very well—perfectly and continually, not just occasionally, dabbling in practice.

By contrast, inner tantra practitioners may achieve the highest realization, full awakening, in one body and one lifetime. This result may even be obtained in half a lifetime, at the moment of death, or in the *bardo*.

The mandalas of the outer and inner tantras are also distinguished by their different characteristics. Deities that are visualized as solitary figures belong to the outer tantric class. Deities that are visualized in union, *yab yum*, characterize the inner tantric class. Deities that wear flowing silk scarves, skirts and beautiful jeweled ornaments belong to the outer tantric class. Deities that wear rosaries made of human skulls, bone ornaments and skin garments belong to the inner tantric class.

Outer and inner tantra practitioners practice in different specific environments. Outer tantra practitioners go to solitary, isolated places, like forests far away from anyone or to the peak of Mt. Meru. Inner tantra practitioners practice anywhere—in cemeteries or in the middle of the busiest city. It does not matter where they practice.

The three inner tantras are *maha, anu* and *atiyoga*. The main focus of mahayoga is kye rim. Anuyoga works with the aspect of transmission and movement as well as with the dissolution of characteristics. Dzogchen atiyoga unites the two.

If we look at the three inner tantras by way of foundation, path and result, mahayoga is the cause for anuyoga, and anuyoga is the result of mahayoga. Likewise, anuyoga is the cause of atiyoga and atiyoga is the result of anuyoga. We could also say that both maha and anu are the cause and ati is the result.

What is the nature and result of atiyoga? It is realization of the *tathagatagarbha*, the innate buddha nature that we all possess. Of the three kayas, the Dharmakaya is the result of atiyoga. Each inner tantric path results in the practitioner's realization of one of the three kayas.

This is a teaching about mahayoga, the inner tantric approach to the generation stage—kye rim. The whole point of receiving and practicing the teachings is to understand your buddha nature, which is the very essence of your being. This understanding comes through practice. If we lacked the buddha nature, what would be the point of the practices? Why would we practice these complicated techniques, and learn the symbolism, if the buddha nature was not already within us, waiting to be revealed? It would be ridiculous to practice if our true nature were not what it is. It would be like pressing a rock to get oil. The effort would be fruitless.

Yet, we must make efforts to realize our buddha nature, even though we all possess it. Just as you would not know that butter is the essence of milk unless you churned the milk—and not just a few churns will do; you really must churn with effort—in the same way, you must practice with effort and diligence to understand your own true nature. Nevertheless, you must remember that practice only reveals what is already present. If you churn water hoping to get butter, it will not happen, will it? We undergo the hardships of the spiritual path because our essence is already Buddha. It is already perfectly realized. If it were not, practice would be pointless. The process is like refining ore that you know has gold in it. You work long and hard to extract the gold from the rock, but if you knew the rock had no gold in it, why would you try to extract it?

Samantabhadra (Tib. Kuntuzangpo), the primordial Buddha, and Buddha Shakyamuni both said that the tathagatagarbha, the buddha essence, is intrinsically present in all animate beings. It is not that some have it and some do not. Every creature that lives has the buddha essence.

If this is so, is there any difference between buddhas and sentient beings? There is one difference, but it is not in their true nature. Every being is Buddha. Buddhas, however, have applied the methods and realized their true nature. They have become buddhas by purifying all their obscurations and karmic afflictions. They have removed all negative habits through joyous effort (Tib. *brtson 'grus*, pronounced "tsondru") and by applying different techniques and practices. Although sentient beings desire happiness and the state of freedom and bliss, they continue accumulating negative causes, obscurations and karmic afflictions. They just sink deeper into ignorance which is the lack of awareness of their true nature. That is the only difference between buddhas and sentient beings.

This situation is analogous to the way we perceive the sun in the sky. We know it is daytime when the sun is in the sky, yet we cannot always see the sun directly—often it is covered by clouds. We cannot see the buddha nature within us when it is covered by the thick clouds of obscurations. What removes the clouds from the face of the sun? The wind. The techniques and practices of maha, anu and atiyoga are like the wind which removes the clouds that obscure the buddha nature. If there were no sun to start with, why would we want to remove the clouds?

When you practice these kye rim practices, it is extremely important to know that there is a result and what the result is. When you begin these practices, you should be aware of the result that you seek to achieve.

CHAPTER II

The General Preliminaries

This text is a commentary to the text entitled *A Clear Explanation of the Stages of Development that Occur During the Time of Practicing and Generating the Deity and Mandala*. All scriptures, commentaries and treatises have a title and, in the Buddhist tradition, each word of the title is a commentary in itself. By simply looking at the title, an excellent scholar would be able to determine all the information contained in the book. Similarly, a scholar of middling scope would be able to determine to which vehicle and class of tantra the text pertained. A scholar of small scope would at least be able to remember the title, as well as have a general understanding of what the text contained.

After the title, as in all texts of this type, there is the homage. As is traditional in the inner tantras, the author offers prostration and homage to the lama, rather than to the buddhas and *bodhisattvas*.

Next is the commitment, which states why the author wrote the text and the commitment that he intends to fulfill through the writing of the treatise. He states his commitment as: "The essence of all living beings is the buddha nature, and this nature is naturally symbolized by the mudra of the deities. By practicing kye rim, the path of Buddha Vajradhara (Tib. Dorje Chang), all ordinary appearances are gathered together and seen as the mudra of the deity. Ordinary structures are perceived as celestial mansions, environments are seen as the deities' mandalas, and beings are seen as deities possessing illusory forms. When one becomes free of phenomena by surrendering belief in true existence and abandons the grasping mind, one sees the true nature of phenomena as the manifestation of illusion. When this wisdom is achieved then one is practicing tantra, which is the union of conventional and ultimate truth. Wisdom is the realization of these two truths, united. In the inner tantras, the anuttara yoga tantra means 'the yoga which is unsurpassed.' A person relies on his personal deity to achieve the common and uncommon spiritual attainments very quickly."

The author of this text was a great scholar from Kathog Monastery named Tsewang Chogdrup. He has written this text to elaborate the important point of relying on and generating one's personal deity. It is presented in a very simple way so that the main points can be comprehended easily. He also mentions that, if you want to study mahayoga in more detail, innumerable treatises upon the subject can be found in both the *kama* and *terma* traditions, as well as in the commentaries written by many venerable masters of the past. Finally, he says this short book covers only the main points of mahayoga; it is not meant to cover everything there is to know about mahayoga.

The result of practice is the realization of the spontaneous, true nature of mind, the perfectly pure, ultimate Truth being. As the result of practice, the practitioner knows this perfect foundation and remains naturally in that state. At the moment of understanding, you realize that you hold the gold in your hand; you see the sun directly, free from obscurations.

Some of you may ask, "Why do we need this purification process? Why do we need the methods and practices when the actual foundation and result are already perfectly pure?" The question is also the answer. As soon as you know your true, perfect nature, whenever that time may be—perhaps tonight, or in the morning—you will not need to practice or be concerned with the objects and methods of purification. You will not need to be concerned with the fourfold process of purification because you will already be in a state of pure, primordial awareness. Until then, you will continue to have many, many disturbing thoughts and concepts. Until these disturbances are pacified, you would do yourselves a favor to rely upon the fourfold process of the practice, find the object to purify, and achieve the result.

Some of you might also ask, "Doesn't a view that negates cause and result actually contradict the Mahayana?" It does not. The Mahayana path consists of the three elements of foundation, path and result. An aspiring tantric practitioner who lacks knowledge of the foundation, path and result before beginning the generation stage of tantric Buddhism will obtain no results. There is no contradiction here. It is essential to properly understand the teachings on the process of purification, the object of purification, and the result of purification. These are the main themes that accompany the practice of the generation stage.

There are three divisions to the practice of kye rim: the preliminaries, the actual practice, and the completion. The first division has two subdivisions: the general preliminaries and the specific preliminaries.

One performs the general preliminaries by developing the Mahayana intention and engaging in the vehicle of the bodhisattvas. One who wishes to enter into tantric practice must develop the mind and conduct of a bodhisattva, a being who possesses ultimate compassion. One develops the Mahayana intention by remembering that, in past lifetimes, all sentient beings have at one time or another been one's own kind and loving parents. Thinking of their kindness, and of the hardship that all living creatures have undergone for your sake and of what you have undergone for their sake, generate the awakened mind of love and compassion. You must do more than simply mouth words; you must give rise to very deep love and compassion for these beings, love which is like the fire that burns the universe at the end of an eon.

Put yourself in the place of a parent looking on his or her only child and think about the kind of care and concern this parent would feel for that child. Thinking in this way, be aware of the kind of love that all beings have had for you in the past and will have for you in the future.

Feeling love that is burning like a great fire, generate the desire to constantly work for the welfare of others. This should be your sole motivation for practice; never lose this intention. You should carry the burden of others' suffering upon your back at all times, and always maintain the unsurpassable state of the awakened mind. It is not suitable to be without it.

For example, without medicine even a very skillful doctor would find it difficult to cure illness. Likewise, without the medicine of compassion, the most important element of Dharma practice, practice will not generate any benefit. Similarly, people in a country suffering famine are not helped by having many weapons to protect themselves in time of war. The most powerful weapon to ensure a country's survival is food and drink. In the same way, if your intention is to achieve enlightenment, liberation, the ultimate state of true happiness, and to share that happiness and work for the welfare of others, you cannot achieve this goal merely by practicing tantric techniques. You cannot succeed without having mastered *bodhicitta*. Without the awakened mind of love and compassion, practicing the generation stage and other kinds of meditations will only make you tired; and in the end you will not have achieved anything, much less liberation. Just as food provides strength to act in the world, compassion provides strength to follow the spiritual path. Nothing else can compare with it and nothing else will work.

There is no living creature that does not desire happiness, yet nearly all continue to create the causes that result in suffering. They continually contradict their own wishes. The tantric methods of the generation stage are swift methods, but they succeed only by engaging the Mahayana mind of bodhicitta. The Mahayana motivation is the foundation of the Vajrayana achievement. You must develop the awakened mind of compassion for all living beings. Lacking this mind, you might as well perform only Hinayana practices, the lesser spiritual pursuit, which does not address the needs of other beings. Then you could achieve some results, although you would not achieve liberation. Practicing for countless eons, you would eventually accumulate enough merit to develop compassion; and, in that state of awareness, eventually you would achieve liberation, but only then. The techniques of the lesser spiritual pursuits consume eons of time and eventually result only in the development of compassion.

The impulse that produces perfect enlightenment—which is the unsurpassable state of unchanging happiness and the ability to share that with others—is awakening your mind to compassion. Similarly, having personal desires and desiring to achieve realization only for your own sake causes all kinds of suffering.

A person who practices the generation stage without having the prerequisite of compassion is neither a Hinayanist nor a Mahayanist and certainly not a Vajrayanist. One who develops compassion and holds the bodhisattva vows prior to practicing Tantrayana will be fully endowed. For such a person the Vajrayana will grow as a perfect stem from the root of the Mahayana. This person has the potential and power to receive any Vajrayana empowerment and can enter any secret mandala, specific or extraordinary. This person can rely on any meditational deity that the spiritual teacher sees fit to give and can hold all three sets of vows with no problem. Such a suitable vessel can truly achieve the results of Vajrayana practice.

The Four Thoughts

Some students might ask, "There are the Mahayana vows of a bodhisattva and there are the Vajrayana vows we receive during empowerment, but what about the Hinayana vows, those of the lesser spiritual pursuit? Did we receive them?" Hinayana vows relate to the renunciation that results from contemplating the Four Thoughts that Turn the Mind: the precious human body; impermanence of sentient beings and of all phenomena; the infallible law of cause and result; and the suffering of cyclic existence. These contemplations and the renunciation of worldly life are the root vows of the Hinayana. They invariably precede the Mahayana and Vajrayana vows. A generation stage practitioner must additionally keep the tantric root and branch words of honor (Skt. *samaya*) very purely and rely on them as a way of life. If you do this, you will be able to apply your understanding of these vows to your generation stage practice, and you will be able to achieve the accomplishments.

It is important to keep three things in mind when you practice the generation stage and to understand why they are indispensable prerequisites: the renunciation of suffering and worldly pursuits that waste time; refuge, the cornerstone of all Buddhist practice; and the awakened mind of bodhicitta.

Renunciation, the first of these three, is achieved by contemplating the Four Thoughts. First, consider that you have obtained the precious human rebirth, this unique occasion, and how valuable it can be if you put it to use. Then realize that it is impermanent and that, with the suddenness of a lightning bolt, it can be taken from you. Then consider the infallible law of cause and result. Have perfect confidence that this law will never fail to be true and realize that, in your karmic condition, whether you have been born in good or bad circumstances, the only experience you will have, now and in the future, is one of suffering. It is the only thing you could possibly experience.

Some say there is happiness in samsara; human beings, even dogs, have moments of bliss and happiness. True, this phenomena is valid but also temporary. When the clouds move aside to reveal the sun, you say the sun is shining and you experience a happy moment. But this situation inevitably changes as another cloud comes to cover the sun again. Beings in cyclic existence can never find permanent, true happiness. Any happiness experienced is temporary, as is their suffering. Both change. Victory and defeat are equally temporary. Events in cyclic existence change like a turning wheel, going from extreme to extreme. In this state of existence there are no permanent, lasting experiences. You can understand the truth of this right now, in this lifetime, if you think just a little deeper than usual.

Through the power of contemplation you can reach the point where you will not want to remain in this state for even one more moment. You lack true happiness because you are in samsara, yet as soon as you depart from samsara you will certainly obtain true happiness. You will only transform your present situation by practicing Dharma and understanding the truth. Develop this attitude by contemplating the Four Thoughts.

Each particular sadhana contains verses that take you through these contemplations. Whether you recite the words or not, you must consider these thoughts before you begin the formal sadhana practice.

Those who want to can consider the Four Thoughts that Turn the Mind in more detail by reading the longer preliminary practices. Those of you who read Tibetan can find the Four Thoughts covered very extensively in many texts, such as the *Yonten Dzod* (Tib. *Yon tan mdzod*) and *Kunzang Lamai Shal-lung* (Tib. *Kun bzang bLa ma'i shal lung*). Contemplate these thoughts carefully and you will become a suitable vessel to practice Dharma. If you are dishonest and crooked, these thoughts will cause you to become very straight and true. Whatever problems you have will immediately clear up by contemplating these truths. And you will not need a teacher either. By contemplating these Four Thoughts, changes will occur on their own.

Refuge

Whether you are practicing in the Hinayana, Mahayana, Sutrayana or Tantrayana, your practice cannot begin without refuge. It is the cornerstone of Buddhist practice.

First, remember that samsara is like a fire pit where the weak, motherly sentient beings, who at one time or another have been your kind and living parents, are lost and tormented. Then awaken the extraordinary mind of compassion, the Mahayana motivation, and kindle the desire to liberate all beings from suffering. Finally, take refuge to benefit all motherly sentient beings who are in cyclic existence and who desire happiness and liberation yet create the causes for more suffering.

One should only take refuge in a perfect source—do not be drawn to impure objects of refuge. Worldly powers and gods, though powerful, attractive and able to teach, are not perfect teachers because they still have traces of obscurations. They are imperfect objects of refuge. They do not have the power to liberate you because they are not liberated.

Imperfect teachers can show you the wrong path. They can cause you to deviate from the true path to liberation and lead you on a path which would only result in worldly power. By following mistaken paths, you may fall to one of the two extreme views of eternalism or nihilism. Such paths are called "wrong spiritual paths" and do not lead to liberation. You should completely reject the idea of taking refuge in imperfect teachers because such a refuge will never result in ultimate, permanent happiness.

As a Buddhist, the Three Jewels of Buddha, Dharma and Sangha are the ultimate source of refuge. Recognizing the jewel of the Buddha as your guide, the jewel of the Dharma as your path, and the jewel of the Sangha as your true companions, these sources of refuge open the way to liberation. Take refuge by recognizing the Three Jewels in this way.

Taking the Buddha as a pure object of refuge means taking refuge in a teacher who is absolutely liberated from cyclic existence and who shows the true path. Taking refuge in the Dharma means taking refuge in a path which leads to perfect enlightenment. Taking refuge in the Sangha means taking refuge in the spiritual companions who pursue the true path to liberation and who avoid mistaken paths.

In the Vajrayana, the student takes refuge in an extraordinary manner by taking refuge in the Three Roots: *lama, yidam* and *dakini*. The lama's nature is actually that of the Three Jewels of refuge; the yidam, or meditational deity, is the refuge of the Buddha; and the dakinis and *dharmapalas* are the refuge of the Sangha.

The great mandala of the Vajrayana practice incorporates the three sources of refuge in the following way: the yidam is understood to be the Buddha and guide on the path who presents the path of appearance and emptiness through the *mandala mudra* (which is the appearance of the deity and the pure land of illusory appearance). The teaching, the Dharma, is that which the mandala mudra expresses. The Sangha are the *dakas* and dakinis who comprise the deity's entourage.

The Three Jewels of refuge and the Three Roots should also be understood to be the one essence of the guru. It is appropriate to recognize the guru in this way and to have fervent regard for this one object of refuge, who is like a wish-fulfilling jewel. A quote from the tantras states: "The guru is the Buddha and the Dharma and Sangha too. The guru is the victorious Vajradhara."

In the space in front of you, visualize a very broad, spacious jewelled throne supported by snow lions. Seated in the center of the throne is your root guru in the form of Vajradhara, the primordial Buddha. Imagine that Vajradhara, who represents your root guru in every respect, is surrounded by the gurus and lamas of all three lineages: the lineage of mind-to-mind transmission, the lineage of symbolic indication, and the lineage of oral transmission.

Directly in front of you and just below and in front of these sacred beings, visualize your own extraordinary meditational deity (yidam) surrounded by the deities from the four or six (depending on how they are counted) tantric classes.

To the right of Buddha Vajradhara (his right) imagine the presence of the buddhas of the three times. One thousand and two buddhas will appear in this glorious light eon. These buddhas appear as the precious jewels of the Buddha.

Behind Vajradhara imagine all the volumes of Buddhist scriptures emblazoned with the vowels and consonants of the Sanskrit language (AH LI KA LI: see Appendix I) and spontaneously resonating with the sounds of the vowels and consonants.

Standing to the left of Vajradhara, in a vast assembly, imagine all of the chief spiritual sons, the spiritual arhats, the supreme sangha members of the Mahayana path and the eight and sixteen bodhisattvas. Surrounding them are the sangha members on the Mahayana path, the path of accumulating merit and preparation, and also the Hinayana members from the *shravakayana* and *pratyeka-buddhayana* (hearers and solitary realizers).

Surrounding all this visualize a vast assembly of dakas and dharmapalas gathered together like thick, massing clouds. All the objects of refuge in this extensive visualization possess omniscient wisdom, compassion, power and other boundless qualities. Regard them as supreme guides to an unknown place. Vividly imagine them to be actually manifesting in the space in front of you.

Next, imagine that your earthly mother and father are sitting next to you and that your actual and formless enemies (such as afflicting spirits and ill omens) appear in front of you. Finally, visualize the sentient beings of the three realms (formless realm, subtle-form realm and desire realm) covering the foundation of the earth in every direction. With palms pressed together, imagine vividly that you are all going for refuge.

Now recite the refuge verses which state, "From this moment, until the supreme state of awakening, when the essence of buddhahood is achieved, I rely upon you. I offer my body, speech and mind to you. I have no other source of refuge than you." Thinking in this way, with intense fervent regard and holding the visualization, recite the verses of your sadhana three times or until you feel satisfied that your prayer is fulfilled.

When you experience a feeling of completion, begin the stages of dissolution—the dzog rim, or completion aspect of the visualization. First, you and all sentient beings dissolve into the objects of refuge. Then, the vast mandala of the objects of refuge gradually dissolves into the central figure, Vajradhara, beginning at the periphery of the mandala and merging toward the center. Rest with Vajradhara in a state without thought. Rest without even the thought of "no thought." Vajradhara is there and nothing else. Rest in a state of meditative absorption on the nature as it is, on the meaning of ultimate truth.

This commentary, being rather brief, does not mention that you should visualize the deities seated on the five branches of the refuge tree; however, you should visualize the tree if possible. You should perform the refuge visualization in exactly the same way as you do in your ngöndro.

If you cannot effect the extensive visualization due to the difficulty, or for whatever reason, then first begin the practice and try to imagine, stage by stage, all the different objects of refuge. Then, as you begin prostrations or recite the verses of refuge, continue to be aware of the presence of the guru as Vajradhara. Under the circumstances that would be sufficient.

For the purpose of accumulating the repetitions that you must perform as part of your ngöndro, you can recite the verses of refuge and bodhicitta as you simultaneously perform one prostration. But do this only if they are short verses that can be recited in the same time it takes to perform one prostration. Then, by the time you finish 100,000 prostrations, you will have also finished 100,000 recitations of the refuge and the bodhicitta prayers. In this way you can complete three parts of the preliminary practice simultaneously.

Going for refuge is the foundation for all further training on the spiritual path. It is also the support for all vows. It is the internal entry to the path of liberation, like being admitted to school. It is the perfect way to practice the Buddhist path. The merit arising from this practice is inconceivable.

In general, you should recite the verses of refuge six times per day. This means twice in the morning, twice at noon and twice at night.

When you take refuge you assume several other commitments. You vow to have total trust in the Three Jewels at all times and to abandon the mind of doubt and hesitation which thinks, "Do I really believe or not?" You must also always respect any image of the Buddha, regardless of size, and all scriptures or printed material which contain Dharma teachings. You should pay homage and make offerings to all true objects of refuge and abandon any lack of respect for these objects.

Once you have taken refuge in the guru, follow your teacher's advice and do whatever he or she instructs you to do without deviation. Having taken refuge in the Buddha, it is no longer permissible to make prostrations or homage to worldly deities or gods. Having gone for refuge in the Sangha, you should no longer befriend people who look down on and doubt the true teachings and words of the Buddha, who doubt your guru or who deny the truth.

The vows and advice mentioned here can be kept quite easily if you know the meaning of refuge. If you know what qualities the objects of refuge represent, it is very easy to go for refuge, to have respect, to keep your vows and to do every other thing you need to do to maintain the practice. Then it is easy to keep the vows as a natural result of your deep, well-founded respect for the sources of refuge.

However, if you do not understand the true meaning of refuge, keeping the vows is very difficult. If someone urges you to take refuge, do the practice and keep the vows and you do so but fail to understand the purpose of it all, later it will be very easy to change your mind. To follow without knowing is not the way. If you carefully examine the qualities of refuge with sincerity, maturity and intelligence, receive the teachings and proceed without rushing or becoming over-anxious, you will gain wisdom and knowledge such as you have never before even touched upon in this life. That is certain.

The problem is that our lives are much too short. If we lived a thousand years, we would never exhaust the lessons to be learned from the Buddha's teachings. The lessons and realizations simply become deeper and more profound. If you studied forever, the wealth of the teachings could not be exhausted. They are like a great ocean. The time never comes when nothing is left to be learned. The depth of wisdom that can be derived from these teachings has no limit.

Bodhicitta

The next preliminary is the practice of bodhicitta that is performed to develop true compassion, the awakened mind. Bodhicitta is discussed in two stages: the meaning and the actual meditation.

Since time without beginning sentient beings have possessed, as their true nature, the primary seed of buddhahood; but because of ignorance, they are unaware of their true nature. Ignorance sets up a play between subject and object and generates a state of endless confusion that is like a turning wheel. Not one of the countless motherly sentient beings lost in this state of utter confusion lacks the desire for happiness.

Unfortunately, sentient beings wish for something entirely different from what they get because they create only the causes for more suffering. Sentient beings have become rather crazy, so you must develop intense mercy and compassion for all of them. You must develop a commitment to help them cross the ocean of suffering and achieve the unsurpassable state of permanent happiness. This compassion is the generation of bodhicitta—the awakened mind.

Since all sentient beings are somewhat crazy and you are numbered among them, you can all be considered equal. You do not understand the causes of either happiness or suffering; otherwise, you would understand why you live in suffering and how to obtain happiness. You would understand what life is all about, what you should abandon and what you should accept to achieve permanent happiness.

It is not sufficient to merely think about this predicament in which you are all stuck. To place other beings in a state of liberation, you must achieve liberation yourself. You cannot help anyone unless you have power, can you? Your commitment must be deep. By dedicating yourself to the liberation of others, you awaken the "aspirational compassion," and your wish to achieve liberation becomes focused on the needs of others.

When you actually apply this aspiration, it is called the "practical application." Practical application is developed by accomplishing the generation stage practice and developing yourself as the deity. Practicing the sadhana is the profound, swift path to fulfill this practical aspiration.

By applying these two extraordinary techniques, the aspiration and the practical application, the perfectly pure bodhicitta is awakened in your mind. Recite the verses of your sadhana three or however many times it takes, until you feel satisfied that you have generated true bodhicitta.

The very moment you develop this compassion you become a son or daughter of the Buddha. Whatever virtue or good karma you have accomplished, be it great or small, becomes measureless. All the negative karma you have accumulated in the past is instantly exhausted. The problems of your life, like sickness, physical obstacles and obstacles to fulfilling your practice, are instantly removed.

You begin to walk the path of liberation the moment you develop bodhicitta. Actually, you begin to walk the path for yourself and others, and the benefits of this are immeasurable. *The Sutra of the Sugatagarbha* states: "How can you measure the merit of generating bodhicitta? If you put it into a form, even the sky is not large enough to contain it." Those who take the bodhisattva vow are counseled never to abandon the mind that hopes to benefit other living beings. Do not get tired and stop practicing because someone offends you; do not abandon such a person. If you lose the bodhicitta, you lose the aspiration and the practice. You cut the practical application from the root so you are left without a foundation. You break the root of the Mahayana, and there is no other method to achieve enlightenment. You should be intensely aware of how important it is to have the awakened mind and never forget it.

Those on the Hinayana path consider the vows of discipline to be the most important. You must understand that here, in the vehicle of the bodhisattvas, the main vow is to develop bodhicitta.

This completes the instructions on the general preliminaries which are performed in all Vajrayana sadhanas. Now we proceed with the actual foundation of the practice beginning with the specific preliminaries.

CHAPTER III

The Specific Preliminaries

The specific preliminaries in the actual sadhana are twofold: (1) clearing away non-conducive circumstances and obstacles and (2) generating and increasing the conducive conditions for practice.

Clearing Away Non-conducive Circumstances

The first specific preliminary, clearing away non-conducive circumstances and obstacles, contains two divisions: (1) expelling negative and demonic forces and (2) establishing the wheel of protection or border of demarcation.

Expelling Negative and Demonic Forces

Begin the meditation from the point of the true nature of reality as it is, the true empty nature of all *dharmas* (perceived objects). Recognizing the actual nature of emptiness, you see the display; seeing the appearances, you realize they are empty. Emptiness is appearance; appearance is emptiness. Like a bubble rising from the water, your self-nature arises as a supreme wrathful deity. This wrathful deity can be Hayagriva or another heruka of your choice. Clearly visualize yourself as the wrathful deity, but do not take the term "wrathful" literally. You appear in the form of enlightened awareness, the display of compassion, substanceless, like the reflection in a mirror.

As for the size of the visualization, since it arises from emptiness, which is the true nature of the mind, open and without any limitation, it can be as large as the three thousand myriads of universes or minutely microscopic. The important point is to strive to perfect a clear visualization.

Next clearly visualize the torma that you will offer to the obstructing forces and then recite the three vajra syllables OM AH HUNG three times (see Plate I).

Reciting OM clears away all impure, dualistic concepts, such as clinging to appearances and thinking they have true inherent existence. AH increases the offering materials, mental and physical, and causes them to become immense and countless in number. HUNG is a wish-fulfilling blessing that causes all desirable qualities, such as color, smell, taste and touch, to arise as an offering to the sense fields. Contemplate this when you recite these three syllables.

At the end of OM AH HUNG, recite HO (see Appendix II). At the sound of HO, all the materials that have been offered and wished for, that have appeared through the blessings of the vajra syllables but could still be exhausted, become inexhaustible. This inexhaustible aspect refers to the nature of appearance of primordial wisdom. Seeing the offerings this way makes them inexhaustible.

Now that you have prepared the perfect offering to the obstructing forces, light radiates from your heart in the aspect of hook-shaped rays with magnetic hooking power that summon and draw in all the negative forces and negative beings. This practice of summoning is different from using light rays to invoke the buddhas and bodhisattvas from their pure lands, where the light from your heart radiates as an offering. In this practice, the hooking instantly magnetizes all negative forces and brings them before you.

Having summoned them, you give them all of the magnificent offerings that you projected, which delight the six sense fields of sight, sound, smell, taste, touch and cognition. Feel that the beings gathered receive equal, sufficient shares; no one gets more or less than another. Since the offerings are inexhaustible there is plenty for the entire gathering.

The obstructing forces and negative beings who have been hooked, who oppose the Dharma, now partake of whatever is needed to satisfy them. Feel certain that every one of them becomes satisfied. These beings have now succumbed to you and are ready to listen to whatever orders you give. Then, with confidence that the obstructing forces have been fully subdued, recite the verses that relate to this visualization.

Next, take the torma, which you offered to expel the negative forces, and throw it out (see Plate II). Order the negative forces to take whatever they have acquired and retreat to their own abode. Repeat the corresponding mantra found in your particular sadhana.

The negative forces then depart, but just in case any still remain intending to create obstacles for your practice, to insure their swift and complete departure, perform the next visualization. From the seed syllable in your heart, light like a burning fire radiates into the ten directions. This light contains countless vajra weapons and tiny replicas of your self-nature as the heruka. Light, weapons and images of yourself pour forth abundantly from the seed syllable, permeating space in every direction, like drops shining in the rays of the sun. This emanation of wrathful energy annihilates all remaining negative forces. Feel convinced that all negativities and obstructing forces, without exception, are destroyed—killed and consumed in flame until not even a name remains.

When you hear words like "kill" and "destroy," do not think of ordinary phenomena like murder or warfare. These visualization techniques destroy negative forces and obstacles through the application of wisdom, not delusion. The principal obstructing force is ego-grasping.

Establishing the Wheel of Protection

Now you have eliminated all obstructing forces. Next, establish the wheel of protection. This is like establishing a line of demarcation or a border. This practice is somewhat like taking steps to protect your environment from a thief.

The vajra weapons that radiated in all directions return and meld together, forming a foundation of solid vajras. The entire earth around you is made of solid blue vajras that have melded together so perfectly that there is no space between them.

Arising from this vajra foundation and perfectly encircling it is a vajra fence made of vertical, horizontal and enmeshed vajras. In the middle of the vajra fence, binding it like a belt, is a rosary of vajras. A vajra canopy, very high and extremely expansive, surmounts the entire arrangement like an immense conical roof.

The vajra fence surrounds you in all directions and the canopy is above. A lattice-like framework of vajras surrounds that. Exterior to the vajra fence and lattice framework is a woven rope-like cord made of vajras. At the very top, in the center of the roof, half of a large vajra stands upright, like a steeple.

There are vajras everywhere. Miniature vajras fill the space in between the large vajras. There is not a single space without a vajra. The vajras are perfectly meshed together, solid blue in color. The vajra weapons and tiny wrathful deities previously emanated are outside this great vajra tent and fence, falling like drops of rain, powerful and in continual motion.

Beyond this falling rain of wrathful deities and weapons, completely surrounding the entire visualization, are masses of blazing fire that consume the universe at the end of the eon. This fire is the display of primordial wisdom. Outside the wisdom fire is the vajra water—inconceivably vast waves constantly pounding together. The water is so powerful it immediately destroys any object that approaches. Outside the vajra water blows the vajra wind. It is sharp like a razor and violent like a hurricane. It cuts any object that approaches.

This wheel of protection is comprised of five circles. As you visualize all this, you should feel that you have created a boundary which prevents all obstructing forces and negativities, and even persons entertaining irrational doubts, from coming near you. They no longer have any power over you.

Imagine yourself within this wheel of protection, with your protectors, mandala and the entire assembly of beings and other practitioners. Your sadhana will prescribe verses that you should recite while visualizing this encircling wheel of protection.

This visualization does more than shut the door to demonic or negative forces. Symbolically, it separates you from ego-grasping. It marks the distinction between the states known as samsara (the mind of cyclic existence, discursive thoughts and especially ego-grasping) and *nirvana* (mind's nature beyond dualistic sorrow).

The five circles symbolize the five primordial wisdoms, which are the actual nature of the five poisons from which ego-grasping is born. The vajra wheel of protection symbolizes a transformation, a separation from this ego so that, from this point throughout the rest of the sadhana, you are practicing in a state of primordial wisdom rather than ego-awareness.

Meditation upon the ultimate wheel of protection is achieved by resting in the state of awareness that realizes that the subject protecting, the object protected and the protection, all three, are empty of true, inherent existence. Resting in a state of non-conceptual wisdom awareness concerning these three recognitions is to effect the ultimate wheel of protection.

If you cannot relate to this empty view of subject, object and act of protection, then effect the ultimate wheel of protection by relaxing in the fresh, natural state of your own pristine presence-awareness itself. Meditating without contrivance is sufficient. Many techniques involve symbolism and visualization and at the end we always rest in the ultimate wisdom nature. Then we do more visualization, again with awareness of the true nature.

This concludes the meditation on the wheel of protection and the visualization that clears away all non-conducive conditions. It also completes the first section of the extraordinary preliminaries.

Establishing Conducive Conditions

The second of the extraordinary preliminaries is the establishment of conducive conditions. This meditation has two parts: (1) the descent of the blessings and (2) blessing the offering materials.

Descent of the Blessings

When you finish the last practice, you cease to visualize yourself as a wrathful deity and begin the practice which establishes the conducive conditions in your ordinary form. Direct your fervent devotion towards the Three Roots—lama, yidam and dakini—and see their qualities of compassion and spiritual power. Suddenly they emanate three types of visualized blessings: their enlightened awareness descends on you in the form of deity images; their enlightened speech descends in the form of mantra syllables; and their enlightened mind descends in the form of hand emblems— vajras, curved knives (Tib. *gri gug,* pronounced "trigug") and other ritual implements which they hold in their hands. The deity images, mantra syllables and hand emblems descend from everywhere and melt into you and your environment, like snow falling into a great lake. Your ritual instruments are blessed, and blessings enter every feature of your environment, removing all impurities.

Recite the appropriate verses from your sadhana while you visualize this descent of blessings. Feel that you have been blessed with the power to assume the form of enlightened awareness, enlightened speech and enlightened mind. This completes the first step, which establishes the conducive conditions. Now proceed to bless the offering materials.

Blessing the Offering Materials

Visualize yourself as the deity. The syllables RAM, YAM and KHAM radiate from your heart (see Appendix II). The syllable RAM, corresponding to the element fire, radiates flame towards all the offering materials that you have gathered and burns away all their impure characteristics. The syllable YAM, corresponding to the element air, blows wisdom air that scatters all clinging to objects as truly existing. The syllable KHAM, corresponding to the element water, pours forth water that cleanses all habitual and negative instincts.

These three elements render your offerings perfectly pure and clean. The samsaric potential attached to your offerings is cleared away through the power of the elements which, in their true nature, are female principles, the three consorts. The first is Dakini Gu Karmo, the second, Dakini Damtsig Drolma and the third, Dakini Mamaki.

In this place of pure offerings see that all material objects are inherently empty, like space. Rest in meditative equipoise and refrain from the tendency to view appearances as truly existing. Thus, you effect the essential offering. In that pure state you can make pure outer offerings of flowers or any other objects that please the five senses.

Next, visualize the syllable BHRUM (see Appendix II), which transforms into an infinitely vast jeweled vessel. Within this vessel is the syllable OM, which brings forth innumerable beautiful flowers from the realm of the gods, that serve as an outer offering. The inner offering is the self-born, natural experience of the five sense fields.

Within this vast jeweled vessel, imagine first the flowers, then all of the different objects that delight the sense fields—water to drink and wash with, perfumed water, food and fragrances—arising and offered by offering goddesses. The whole visualization is magnificent, perfect and unlimited. Every available space is filled with offerings. Thus, ordinary merit is accumulated by making ordinary offerings.

Three specific offerings are made during a Vajrayana sadhana: medicine (Tib. *sman*, pronounced "men"), ritual cake (Tib. *gtor ma*, pronounced "torma") and blood (Tib. *rak ta*). Each offering has a meditation that precedes it.

The first offering requires a container which is self-born. Inside an infinitely vast skull cup (Tib. *thod pa*) is the essence of the five types of flesh and the five types of nectar. The first flesh is human flesh and the first nectar is feces, both of which appear in the center of the skull cup.

In the eastern direction of the skull cup, the flesh of an ox and the nectar semen appear; in the south, the flesh of a dog and the marrow of a human; in the west, the flesh of a horse and menstrual blood; and in the north, the flesh of an elephant and urine appear.

The five fleshes symbolize the five buddhas or five types of primordial awareness. The five nectars symbolize the five consorts and the pure nature of the five elements. Each flesh and nectar is marked by the seed syllable of the buddha and consort. They are: in the center, HRI/PAM; in the east, HUNG/LAM; in the south, TRAM/MAM; in the west, OM/MUM; in the north, AH/TAM (see Appendix II). Then the seed syllables transform into the five buddhas with their consorts.

From the point of union of the five buddhas and consorts, the white and red substances mingle and descend into the skull cup. The white and red nectar fills the skull cup in all directions, dissolving into the five types of flesh and nectar. The fleshes and nectars then dissolve, following which the buddhas and consorts also dissolve, melting into the nectar.

The nectar is now fully endowed with the essence of the color, smell, taste and power of the five states of primordial wisdom. This is the offering of *men*, medicine. This has been an extremely brief explanation.

Next, offer the *torma*. Visualize a jeweled vessel as vast as space with a base the size of the earth. Inside the vessel is the torma. The torma represents whatever it is that you want to offer to the deities. Think that the torma is great and wish-fulfilling, adorned with the sun and moon, filling all of space.

According to tradition, it is often explained here that the jeweled vessel represents the universe, or the inanimate world, and that the torma within, which is offered along with all materials, possessions and wealth, represents all animate sentient beings.

The offering of *rakta* is accompanied by the following visualization: imagine an infinitely vast vessel made of a freshly severed skull. This vessel contains blood, symbolizing the total energy of desire and attachment in the three realms. Since the blood contains the attachment of the three realms, the actual nature of the blood is free from attachment, and its nature is desireless great bliss. Imagine that whatever pure qualities you wish for are contained within the skull cup. Then, recite the corresponding verses from your sadhana.

These three offerings—*men*, torma and rakta—also represent the three kayas of enlightened awareness. The nature of medicine is appearance, the nature of blood is emptiness, and the nature of the ritual cake is the union of the two.

Most sadhanas contain verses for refuge and bodhicitta, but extremely abbreviated sadhanas will not contain these other practices, such as the wheel of protection and the three offerings. Some extremely abbreviated versions even omit refuge and bodhicitta. Often in very abbreviated sadhanas, you will instantly become the deity upon recollection.

We have covered refuge as a preliminary to the sadhana, bodhicitta—which awakens the mind—and the special preliminaries including clearing away non-conducive conditions and creating conducive conditions. These practices are preliminary to the actual sadhana.

CHAPTER IV

The Actual Practice: The Yoga of Meditative Equipoise
Part I

The second part of the practice is the actual sadhana, which has two parts: (1) the yoga of meditative equipoise, and (2) the yoga of arising from equipoise.

The yoga of meditative equipoise has three subdivisions: (1) the yoga of the physical mudra; (2) the yoga of speech, and (3) the yoga of the clear light nature of the mind. The first of these, the yoga of the physical mudra, has five subtopics: (1) penetrating the inner meaning through the three states of meditative absorption, (2) generating the support and supporting mandalas (the celestial mansion and the deities within), (3) invoking the primordial wisdom beings and establishing firm presence, (4) performing prostration, making offerings and rendering praise, and (5) training in meditative concentration upon the generation of the principal deity.

The Yoga of the Physical Mudra

The Three Meditative Absorptions

Turning then to the first of these five subtopics—penetrating the inner meaning through the three states of meditative absorption—we shall begin. The first meditative absorption is the absorption on the nature as it is. Explaining this with reference to the object to be purified, the means of purification and the result thereof: the object of purification is the consciousness at the moment of death; the means of purification is to remain in the awareness of the natural mind; and the result is the experience of the nature of mind free from dualistic sorrow.

If you are not familiar with the stages of dissolution that occur at the moment of death, you can refer to the teachings on the bardo of the moment of death. Studying the bardo teachings, one learns how the elements of the physical body dissolve back into one another. The element earth dissolves into water, water dissolves into fire, fire dissolves into air, and air dissolves into space or consciousness. There are various corresponding outer signs that occur to the dying person. Even without studying these matters, you can clearly see how your body, which is like the element earth, will decay back to its constituent elements.

Death occurs for all sentient beings after the white, red and black flashes of light occur and the consciousness experiences the clear, empty light of ultimate truth. Resting in the first absorption purifies that moment when a sentient being fails to recognize the clear light and thus turns away from liberation.

The meditative absorption on the nature as it is can also be explained by considering the nature of the actual practice or means of purification.

The actual practice is to be aware of the natural mind which is not a created or manufactured dharma. Resting in the equanimity of this direct, fresh natural state of ordinary mind, all dharmas appear to be going nowhere. The sensual appearances—form, sound, smell, taste and touch—are all found to be going nowhere. Not only are they going nowhere, they do not remain in any place at the present moment. There are no concepts at all in the natural state of mind. There are no valid statements of fact. Perceiving this natural state of mind is to rest in the meditative absorption on the nature as it is.

The unborn, unobstructed state of perfect, discriminating awareness—the natural mind—cannot possibly be contrived. If you were asked to state the essential characteristic of this state, you could not say that is exists as an experience. From the very beginning, it has never been something that can be experienced. It is not something which has been created. It would be impossible to refer to a "vajra" if a vajra had never existed. But once a vajra has been known to exist, it is possible to refer to it as an object, even if it were no longer present.

If you ask, "What are the characteristics of the perfect state of meditation on ultimate reality, the true nature of the mind?," the question cannot be answered. Since there have never been any characteristics, it is impossible to describe them. This state of mind cannot be experienced or perceived, since it has no existence and never has had any existence.

Although it has no existence and cannot be experienced, neither can it be said to be nonexistent. You cannot say "it is" because the Buddha never saw it. Nor can you say "it isn't" because it is the very foundation of samsara and nirvana. This truth is not premised on eternalistic or nihilistic views. This truth is empty and void. That which ought to be known about it cannot be rationalized. That the view cannot be described in words proves that it has no definite characteristics. The true nature of our being, our mind, does not lie in compounded or corporeal materials. Therefore, there is nothing on which to fix the emotions.

The nature of mind is symbolically expressed by referring to the three doors of liberation. The first door is that the nature of mind has no existence, the second door is that the nature is unconditioned, and the third door is that the nature is passionless, meaning that there is nothing upon which to fix the emotions.

What is the result of the meditative absorption on the nature as it is? It is gaining the intrinsic awareness of the state of absolute inactivity, ultimate truth itself. This is the meaning of the Dharmakaya Buddha, the ultimate truth being of enlightened awareness.

This discussion really has no external relevance. It is simply a discussion of the nature of pure awareness (Tib. *rig pa*), our own pristine presence.

The object to purify and the result of purification are the same: the foundational state of mind and the result are both the buddha nature. Meditating in this way purifies the moment in the process of death when awareness is impure, the habitual instincts which are associated and the tendency to cling to material existence. This is what is purified initially. Eventually, however, the mind actualizes the clear light nature and is liberated. Applying the practice as a remedy results in nirvana, the experience of the mind beyond sorrow, the ultimate truth being of enlightened awareness and the fruition of the perfect state of full awakening.

The second meditative absorption—the absorption on all appearances—is also explained with reference to the object to purify, the practice of purification and the result. Meditating on appearances from the perspective of truth purifies that moment during the death process that occurs after one has failed to recognize the clear light of the ultimate truth.

At the moment of death, consciousness and vital air enter the Bardo of Intrinsic Reality, during which time the "mental body" will wander about in a dreamlike state. The sense fields are all intact, so one experiences sensual phenomena very quickly. The mental body eagerly chases after all the sensual experiences. The practice purifies this state of fleeting mental impressions.

The practice, then, is to develop a perfect awareness of the true nature of mind. The true nature of mind includes both what we refer to as samsara, cyclic existence, and what we refer to as nirvana, the state beyond sorrow. Resting in the true nature, not seeing samsara and nirvana as separate, and not deviating from this awareness, the intensity of this luminous awareness appears as illusory appearances.

Samsara arises when one thinks that appearances truly exist, that they are not illusory. This is why sentient beings in the six realms of cyclic existence experience all kinds of mental suffering. Thinking that appearances truly exist, when in fact objective appearances are illusory, causes you to wander in samsara, this place without freedom.

The object of purification is purified by developing compassion for the sentient beings in the six realms who must experience this all-pervasive condition of suffering. Developing all-encompassing compassion, which is also transparent and free of grasping or partiality, purifies the object.

As a result of the practice, one realizes the Sambhogakaya, the Illusory Blissful Being, the complete enjoyment being of enlightened awareness. Like the deities who perfectly possess the major and minor marks of enlightenment, one realizes the illusory expression of wisdom.

The bardo body, the object that is purified, and the result again are the same. To see the true nature is to see the illusory nature of all appearances.

If you apply this practice to your own situation in cyclic existence, habitual instincts and stains will be cleared away. Any partiality towards emptiness will also be removed. Eventually you will achieve the Sambhogakaya. The practice plants and nourishes the seed that matures as the Sambhogakaya. As a result, the clear light of wisdom will arise in the form of the deity, the expression of intense compassion. This is the illusory mental body that is the very foundation for the completion stage of Vajrayana practice, called dzog rim. Generating the illusory form, awareness ripens into the completion stage and the ability to practice on higher levels. This completes the explanation of the first two states of meditative absorption.

The third meditative absorption is the absorption on the primary cause. This also is explained with reference to the object to purify, the practice and the result.

The object to purify is the moment in the Bardo of Becoming when the mental body, having already established a particular direction due to previous karmic potencies, is about to be reborn in the realm of cyclic existence. We seek to purify the moment when the mind and vital air are about to enter cyclic existence.

In general, there are five paths to follow to achieve enlightenment: the path of accumulating merit, the path of preparation, the path of seeing, the path of meditation, and the path of no more learning.

The time when the mental body is wandering in the bardo is likened to the path of accumulating merit; the moment when the mind and vital air are about to enter the future body is likened to the path of preparation; the time of conception is likened to the path of seeing; the foetus that is fully formed inside the womb and about to be born is likened to the path of meditation; and birth is likened to the path of no more learning.

The practice that purifies the object is the practice of emptiness and great compassion. These two qualities are brought together in practice. The state of nonobjective pure awareness is symbolized by the seed syllable of the deity. When you see the deity's seed syllable, be aware of its non-corporeal existence; then it becomes a support for bodhicitta, ultimate compassion.

Seed syllables are like the root of life; they are the life of ultimate compassion. They are extremely clear and radiant and never change. Whatever arises from them is suitable to be meditated upon.

HRI is the syllable for Avalokiteshvara; HUNG is the syllable for Vajrakilaya; BAM is for certain other deities and dakinis; and TAM is the syllable for Tara. Sentient beings in the six realms also have seed syllables: NRI is the syllable for humans. All mandalas arise from the seed syllable BHRUM.

The nature of true, ultimate compassion is emptiness. It is not necessary to take compassion and mix it with emptiness, using some formula. The two are indivisible; they have never been two. True compassion is empty of subject and object.

The result of the practice is attaining the Nirmanakaya, the manifestation being of enlightened awareness. Thereby one gains the ability to manifest in any form necessary to help sentient beings.

All of the different tantric deities are symbols of enlightened awareness who appear in order to benefit sentient beings. The deities in union—*yab yum*—do not symbolize desire; they manifest enlightened awareness to cure desire. Likewise, wrathful deities are not an expression of anger or wrath, but instead are an intense expression of the ultimate compassion that has manifested in coarse, illusory form to tame sentient beings impossible to tame otherwise.

Deities in union represent the state of nonobjective awareness, ultimate compassion. The nature of this compassion is emptiness.

The female principle of enlightened awareness is emptiness, and the male principle is compassion or method. These two together, expressed by the deities' union, symbolize this non-dual state.

Meditation upon the seed syllable purifies the primary cause: the moment when the consciousness and the vital air mix and one is reborn into the next realm of awareness. The practice purifies that moment when one is reborn into the world of cyclic existence.

This meditation practice also relates to the vow that the buddhas have taken to manifest in various forms to help sentient beings. The seed syllable is the cause for the birth of all the deities in the mandala and also the cause for the development of the mandala in a general way.

This practice purifies the habitual tendency to take rebirth and helps one directly understand the non-dual nature of appearance and emptiness. Eventually, the actual manifestation being, the Nirmanakaya, results. This practice plants the seed for achieving the Nirmanakaya and complete liberation. It causes the state of bliss to arise from the union of consciousness and vital air. By generating yourself as the deity, you plant the seed which grows into the awareness of bliss, bliss which is born from the union of vital air and the mind. This is the same experience that occurs at the time of dzog rim, the completion stage. As long as the mind and vital air remain in an impure state, one continues to wander in cyclic existence. But working with the pure wisdom air and consciousness purifies the mind so that one arises as the illusory form of the deity.

Generally speaking, these three states of meditative absorption are the foundation for all Vajrayana sadhanas. Since they are the foundation for the generation stage practice, you should understand them clearly when you perform the sadhana. You should never be without these three meditative absorptions. In fact, these three are the foundation for all practices, but since some practices are short and some are long, the three may not be clearly defined in the sadhana. In any case, you must always include them. Next we begin with the actual practice of the mandala generation.

Generating the Support and Supporting Mandalas

The generation of the support and supporting mandalas in the state of enlightened awareness is called the yoga of the mudra of form.

There are three stages in the process of generating the mandala: first, the arrangement of the five elements on top of each other to form the base of the mandala; second, the generation of the celestial mansion; and third, the generation of the seat of the meditational deity.

A mandala is not constructed in the same way that an ordinary house is built. Generating the mandala begins by stacking the elements to form the base. The object that is purified during this process is one's creation of a universe out of the four elements. Our universe is the manifestation of a distorted, relative state of consciousness; it is appearance manifesting through the imperfect activity of mind. You perceive the universe, traditionally said to be comprised of Mt. Meru, the continents and subcontinents, as a solid "physically existing" realm, due to your distorted, relative state of awareness which grasps at duality. You believe that the earth, rocks and external objects concretely exist just as you perceive them; ultimately, they do not. By visualizing the extensive wheel of protection that was presented in the preliminaries and accomplishing the visualization which follows, you purify this distorted view.

The syllable AH appears and then transforms into a blue *dharmadayo* pyramid which is inverted, with three sides and an extremely sharp point. Its shape is like the shape which is left when a phurba has been stuck into the mud and then quickly pulled out. This pyramid is infinitely vast and symbolizes the element space.

On the top of this inverted pyramid, the syllable YAM appears and then transforms into an air mandala. In the center of it is a crossed vajra and circulating around it is dark, blackish green smoke. On top of this, the seed syllable RAM transforms into a red, square, fire mandala encircled by flames. On top of this, the seed syllable BAM appears, which transforms into a water mandala. This mandala is circular and white and is surrounded by white light. Above this, the seed syllable LAM appears, which transforms into an earth mandala. It is gold in color, naturally square, and surrounded by golden light. Above this the syllable SUM appears, which transforms into the four-jeweled Mt. Sumeru: gold, lapis lazuli, ruby and mother of pearl. This is meant to be a vast and expansive visualization.

Next is the generation of the celestial mansion. Here again there is the object to purify, the practice and the result. The object to be purified is the attachment that sentient beings have for material things and places.

The practice begins by intoning the syllable BHRUM (see Appendix II), which descends to land on top of Mt. Meru and then melts into light, causing the celestial mansion to appear. It rests on the very peak of Mt. Meru, which is on top of the five sequentially heaped elements. It appears in the center of the vajra wheel of protection that you have already established in the prior visualization.

The earth is the foundation of the mansion, which is surrounded by a fence made of vajras. An immense five-colored fire surrounds the vajra fence. Within the perimeter of the vajra fence are the eight great cemeteries in a circle (see Plate VI and Appendix 3). Next visualize in the center of the mandala a vast, thousand-petalled white lotus with a vast pollen heart. Upon the pollen heart rests a sun mandala equal in proportion with the pollen heart. Resting atop the sun mandala is a jeweled crossed vajra with a blue-colored square at the center. This forms the base of the celestial palace mandala which is also square.

The celestial mansion has five concentrically arranged walls, formed of five kinds of jewels, each of a different color. If the main deity you are about to generate is white, then the innermost wall is white. If the deity is red, the innermost wall is red, and so on. The other four walls proceed out from the innermost wall.

The first outer level of the mansion has a red landing going all the way around, with sixteen offering goddesses standing upon it. The goddesses face in towards the mansion, holding various wonderful offerings that they offer with mudras.

Jutting forth from the top of the outermost wall is a yellow border inlaid with jewels. Above the border, a series of tiny pillars rise up into the roof. The outside walls are a different color in each of the four directions: the east wall is white, the south wall is yellow, the west wall is red, and the north wall is green.

Within the celestial mansion eight great pillars support four beams. The ceiling is completely covered with jewels, except for an empty space in the very center. The mansion has four entrances, one in each of the four directions. It has a domed roof and red corbels supporting its towers. Each corbel is ornamented with figures of gods bearing offerings of worship to the deities. The corbels support cornices which are blue in the east, yellow in the south, red in the west and green in the north. Each of the four entrances has a pillared portico ornamented with a Dharma wheel, umbrellas, banners, figures of antelopes and yak-tail fans with jeweled handles. A victory banner and an umbrella crown the roof and the entire mansion is decorated with beautiful flowers, gems and banners.

Outside, there are eight great cremation grounds. The first is called "gruesome"; the second "dense jungle"; the third "burning with a 'wur wur' sound"; the fourth, "the terrible cremation ground"; the fifth, "perfectly endowed"; the sixth, "ever gloomy"; the seventh, "resounding with the cries of 'killy, killy' (the shrill cries of eagles and other birds of prey)"; and the eighth, "resounding with the wild laughter of 'ha, ha'." Each of them is adorned with one of the eight kinds of gigantic trees, clouds, rivers, fires and large stupas.

In each cremation ground is a god. In the first is a yellow Indra, mounted on an elephant, holding a thunderbolt. In the second is a yellow Yaksha mounted on a horse holding a mace. In the third is a white Varuna mounted on a makara holding a noose. In the fourth is a blue Yama mounted on a buffalo holding a lance. In the fifth is a red, four armed Agni, mounted on a goat, making the gesture of giving boons with one of his right hands and gripping a three headed mace with his other; his two left hands hold a rosary and a vessel containing drops of wine. In the sixth burning ground, a black Raksha mounted on a zombie body holds a sword and a skull. In the seventh, a green Merut mounted on a deer holds a banner. In the eighth, a white Vengdan mounted on a bull holds a three-pointed thunderbolt. Each god is beautifully dressed, bedecked with jewels, and is accompanied by a consort the same color as himself standing to his left. Each god bows toward the victorious buddhas.

The cremation grounds, according to different practices, are populated with yogis, yoginis, siddhas, vidyadharas, pretas, rakshas, yakshas, ghouls, elementals, dakas and dakinis, jackals and other beings. Imagine that eight of these cremation grounds, filled with these different beings, surround the celestial mansion.

When you visualize the mansion, remember the four entrances, the main pillars and the fact that everything is made of jewels and precious substances. These are the characteristics of a peaceful mandala.

On the other hand, wrathful mandalas, which are generated so that wild beings might be tamed, are terrifying and resemble cemeteries. The walls are made of dry, moist and fresh skulls. The eight pillars are made of the eight great gods. The eight crossbeams are made of the eight great nagas. Covering the ceiling are the twenty-eight constellations of stars that the moon passes through in its revolution.

The windows are made of the sun, moon, and the eight planets. The hanging net is a trellis of snakes and skulls. The rafters are adorned with malas of fingers, skulls, the five organs and the sun and moon. The dome of the roof is made of a great god's skull. On top of the roof, where the umbrella and Dharma wheel would be in the peaceful mandala, there is a heart, a banner and a canopy made from human skin.

The wrathful celestial mansion looks like a burial ground inside and out. Still pools of blood lie everywhere and a black, violent wind is blowing like a tornado. A terrifying firelight pervades the environment.

It is important to think that your visualization is entirely pure and to recollect the true meaning of the symbols. How? By recalling the qualities of enlightened awareness, the qualities of the Buddha—inconceivable compassion and miraculous concerned activity. Think that your entire meditation symbolizes this compassionate and pure concerned activity. This concludes the practice of generating the mandala.

The result of performing this practice is the achievement of ultimate primordial awareness, the natural dharmadhatu. This is undistorted awareness, the great liberation. It is likened to the great womb of the primordial mother and is symbolized by the vast dharmadayo inverted pyramid. The five elements are born from this great womb of emptiness.

The five female consorts, the principles of enlightened awareness, are the true nature of the five elements. They are vast and pure like space. The elements are the mudra—the five consorts—arising from the womb of ultimate truth. The terms "womb" and "mother" refer to the palace of all the buddhas, the place from which all states of enlightened awareness arise.

The true meaning of the various structural portions of the celestial mansion should be understood as follows: the square shape symbolizes the equality of the expanse of ultimate truth. The four entrances symbolize the four immeasurable qualities. The beams stacked on top of each other at the roof symbolize the steps along the path—the eight vehicles. The four roofs symbolize the result of the path and the four essential qualities. The Dharma wheel on the roof symbolizes the continual turning of the Dharma. The bottom step symbolizes the four applications of mindfulness. The four little beams on the roof symbolize the four pure efforts. The four windows at each of the four entrances symbolize the four miraculous legs. The five walls symbolize the five powers: faith, perseverance, mindfulness, single-pointed concentration and wisdom. The seven branches of enlightenment are represented by the frame, net of jewels, rosary of flowers, silken cloth hangings, mirrors, half moon and the yak-tail whisk used for fanning and dusting. The eight pillars symbolize the eightfold path.

The four beams symbolize the four fearlessnesses. The twenty-eight ledges that the roof rafters rest upon symbolize the eighteen states of emptiness and the ten paramitas. The piece of wood forming the edge of the roof symbolizes the inconceivable qualities. The small pieces of wood that support the upper beams symbolize the four states of pure awareness.

The roof of the celestial mansion symbolizes the vast mandala of enlightenment and the truth that buddhahood is one mandala of primordial awareness. The dharmadayo pyramid at the very bottom means the same thing. The umbrella on the roof symbolizes compassion that is sufficiently great to protect all sentient beings. The flag symbolizes mercy.

The light that radiates from the celestial mansion symbolizes the inexhaustible activity of body, speech and mind. The radiance inside and out symbolizes the display of primordial wisdom. The crossed vajras at the bottom symbolize the inseparability of emptiness and primordial wisdom. The twelve prongs on the vajra symbolize the twelve links of interdependent origination that have been purified.

The sun disc symbolizes the natural, clear light of ultimate truth. The lotus symbolizes the quality of remaining unaffected by any fault or stain of cyclic existence. The eight great burial grounds symbolize the purification of the eight states of consciousness. The vajra fence symbolizes the destruction of demonic forces, or delusions.

For one's meditative effort to be pure, it is important to know the meaning of the symbols generated in meditation, whether wrathful or peaceful. Otherwise, due to improper view, one might be reborn as a demon.

If you are a beginner and it is too difficult to remember all that has been said here, then when you meditate, simply be aware that the various aspects of the mandala are representations of the qualities of the mind of enlightened awareness. This thought will ensure a pure practice.

You may also understand the symbolism by considering the elements stacked at the base to represent the essential energy channels and the five chakras. The foundation of the mandala (the lotus, sun and crossed vajra) represents the central channel that contains the vital air and essential fluid, which mingle to form the inconceivable mandala of the clear and empty mind.

When you meditate on the clear, empty nature of mind, the energy channels, the vital air and essential fluid become soft, flexible, unobstructed and pure, thus becoming suitable for practicing the completion stage practices. In this way, the generation stage naturally ripens into the completion stage.

The various aspects of the celestial mansion, from bottom to top, symbolize the threefold aspect of enlightened awareness. They symbolize all of the qualities of the Buddha's form, the thirty-two major and eighty minor marks; all the qualities of the Buddha's speech which are the sixty branches of melodious sound; and all the qualities of the Buddha's mind, the complete understanding of conventional and ultimate truth. These qualities of wisdom, power and compassion all relate to the mind.

Obscurations relating to your physical body can also be purified by visualizing the celestial mansion as representing your own channels, the mansion's ornaments as representing your air, and the deity as representing your essential fluid. The five elements that form the mansion's base relate to the five elements of which your body is composed. Space relates to mind, air to breath, water to blood, fire to heat, and earth to flesh. The deity is born of the union of the white and red seeds within the essential fluid.

Next generate the seat of the deity. Here again, there is an object to purify, a means of purification and the result thereof. The object that you seek to purify is the mode of phenomenal rebirth. Sentient beings are reborn in various ways: through the union of blood and seed (the way human beings are born), through heat and moisture (the way parasites are born), through an egg, or by miraculous appearance. By means of the practice, you purify the actual place of rebirth.

The place of practice is the very center of the celestial mansion. Here, visualize a red lotus seat upon which a red sun and a white moon mandala lie flat. Both the sun and the moon are the same size. Together, the red lotus seat, sun and moon form the seat of the central deity. Peaceful deities sit on a moon disc surmounting a sun disc or void of a sun disc; wrathful deities sit on a sun disc that surmounts a moon disc.

The seats of the other deities in the entourage differ according to different sadhanas. The seats of wrathful deities will have male and female demons, corpses and living beings such as elephants, all of which are symbols of delusion, beneath their feet. By undertaking the visualization of the deity you perform the practice.

As a result of this practice, the meditator achieves the manifestation being of enlightened awareness, the Nirmanakaya. Having attained the Nirmanakaya, you may take rebirth wherever you wish, in incarnations without stain or fault. A being who incarnates in this way is called a "tulku." Because the tulku's mind is naturally perfect and rests in a state of clear light, method and wisdom are perfectly united in his or her mind. This state of primordial awareness, perfectly complete, is the result.

The result of generation stage practice, mahayoga, is entry into completion stage practice, anuyoga. The symbolism of the deity's seat in the context of anuyoga is as follows: the lotus corresponds to the energy channels and wheels. The sun corresponds to the mystic heat, visualized in the shape of a triangle just below the navel. The moon represents the seed from the father, visualized as the white inverted syllable HAM (see Appendix II) in the crown.

By controlling the vital air, the yogi ignites the mystic heat, which then travels up the central channel where it melts the white seed in the crown. This practice ripens into the unchangeable experience of bliss. This completes the teaching on the generation of the deity's seat.

Meditation on the form of the deity is the core of the practice. The deity and the type of visualization you will perform will depend on the kind of sadhana you are doing and the class to which the deity belongs. When you meditate upon the form of the deity, the object that you seek to purify is the bardo consciousness seeking to enter the union of the father's seed and the mother's blood.

The solar seat represents the blood-red egg of the mother, and the lunar seat represents the semen of the father. The descent of the seed syllable, the primary cause for absorption, upon the solar and lunar seats, corresponds to the moment when the bardo consciousness enters the fusion of white and red and conception occurs. The mixing of the red and white substances and the consciousness corresponds to the moment when the seed syllable transforms into the hand emblem which is held by the deity.

Light then radiates from the hand emblem, making offerings to the buddhas. It returns, bearing blessings, then radiates again, penetrating all sentient beings, and returns once more. By visualizing the radiation and reabsorption of light from the hand emblem, the meditator purifies the moment of conception when the consciousness enters the womb. Each cycle of radiation and reabsorption corresponds to a stage in the development of the elements and organs in the womb. The particulars of the phases of growth during the nine months of human gestation are given detailed attention in the more extensive generation stage teachings.

In some practices, the various stages, where the seed syllable transforms into the hand emblem and then into the deity, are subsumed into a single visualization in which the meditator instantly becomes the deity. The moment you recollect the deity you become the deity. This practice purifies miraculous rebirth.

The generation of the deity can be described as follows: the seed syllable simply appears from space, then descends upon the seat, which was previously visualized. This is called the sadhana of the seed syllable and pertains to speech. From the hand emblem, the essence of the seed syllable, boundless light rays emanate, invoking the awareness of the buddhas and inviting them to come before you. The light reabsorbing into the hand emblem completes the sadhana of the hand emblem. This visualization pertains to the mind. The transformation of the seed syllable and the hand emblem into the form of the deity, the diamond being, pertains to the body and completes the sadhana of the fully accomplished form. By accomplishing these practices, the meditator gains the ability to intentionally take rebirth as a tulku to work with and tame the minds of sentient beings still in samsara.

Practicing the generation stage ripens the mind of the meditator, readying it for the completion stage. As previously stated, the lotus, sun and moon seat represent the central energy channel, the various wheels and heat and bliss. Heat melts the seed in the crown, which causes drops of inconceivable bliss to descend from the crown. Step by step, the practitioner experiences the four stages of great bliss, the knotted wheels unwind, and the vital air and mind dissolve into the central energy channel.

In the generation stage practices, the sadhana of the seed syllable and hand emblem correspond to the process of vital air and consciousness dissolving into the central energy channel. In anuyoga, the radiation and reabsorption of light and the transformation of the hand emblem into the perfect form of the deity correspond to the experience of great bliss and empty awareness. This is because the deity's form is the display of primordial wisdom, bliss and emptiness. Thus, the generation stage practice lays the foundation for anuyoga, completion stage practices and attainments.

Whatever the particular details of the visualizations in a sadhana, it is important to perform them correctly. Some short sadhanas may have a seat for the deity but not a celestial mansion. In some practices the deity appears the instant you become aware. This kind of practice is without any contrivance at all—the deity just appears. If the sadhana has no activities, it is meant to be that way. You should understand that the various parts to the practice of generation stage, including the celestial mansion, are not rigidly fixed; no particular form is absolutely required.

The same rule applies when you visualize the essential characteristics of the deity. The characteristics of the yidam are meant to
accord with your particular sadhana. There is no fixed set of
characteristics. What is important is to perceive the deity's pure
meaning.

Next is the appearance of the deity. This subject has two subdivisions: the first is how to generate the deity's form, and the second regards the characteristics of the deity. These subjects are quite
difficult to understand, so special attention will be given to the
details of the transformation of the seed syllable into the hand emblem. To receive the desired purifications and results, it is important to understand how this transformation occurs.

In extensive Vajrayana practices the transformation of the deity
occurs in five stages, in medium-length sadhanas it occurs in four
stages, and in short sadhanas in three. The Nyingmapa tradition,
especially the tradition of terma, or treasures, often makes use of
short sadhanas; though, of course, it makes use of extensive and
medium-length sadhanas as well. In some sadhanas the deity appears instantly; there are no stages at all. This is known as perfection upon instantaneous recollection.

The object that is purified by visualizing the form of the deity is
the stage when the bardo consciousness enters the fusion of blood
and semen at the moment of conception. When you hear the words
"bardo consciousness," you may think they refer to someone else's
bardo consciousness or that all the consciousnesses out there in
the bardo are the objects to be purified. These words refer only to
your own bardo consciousness. Your consciousness has gone
through these various stages of rebirth innumerable times and will
continue to do so. In fact, your consciousness is very, very familiar
with these different stages. These teachings and practices are meant
to purify your own mind as the object of purification.

A peaceful deity always sits or stands on a lunar mandala, which
may or may not have a solar mandala beneath it; wrathful deities
will always sit or stand on a solar mandala, not a lunar mandala.
The solar mandala represents the blood of the mother, and the lunar mandala represents the seed of the father. Conception requires
both, so your visualization must contain both. The solar and lunar
seats resting on the lotus directly relate to the process of the

mother's egg and the father's semen mixing together at the time of their sexual union. The bardo consciousness sees its future mother and father and, because of the karmic force generated by the sexual act, is attracted and enters the fusion of egg and seed. The object that is purified here is the moment when the bardo consciousness enters that fusion.

The seed syllable, the primary cause for meditative absorption, appears next. It descends and comes to rest at a point over the center of the solar and lunar discs. The moment the seed syllable appears it transforms into the hand emblem of the deity. You might wonder, since some deities have many hands and hold many different emblems, how is it determined which emblem to use? The emblem that appears is that which the deity holds in his or her main right hand.

The object that is purified during this visualization is the bardo consciousness mixed with very subtle vital air that has entered the fusion of seed and egg in the womb.

Light radiates from the hand emblem in the form of offerings and then reabsorbs. The number of times the light radiates and reabsorbs, and whether it radiates from the seed syllable or the hand emblem, depends on each particular sadhana.

The egg, seed, consciousness and vital air have mixed together, and the next stage is the gradual development of the four elements into flesh, bones, blood and air. As the foetus grows inside the womb, the sense organs gradually develop until they are complete. The radiation and reabsorption of light purifies the development of the four elements as the sense organs.

The hand emblem then transforms into the complete form of the deity. This visualization directly purifies the process of birth—the baby coming out into the world and starting to cry. The habit of being born into the world is purified by this stage of the visualization.

Beings are also born from eggs, through the fusion of heat and moisture, and by spontaneous, miraculous birth, as when taking rebirth in the god and hell realms. The visualization of the hand emblem transforming into the deity has the power to purify each type of birth.

Birth through an egg is purified in the following way: when the seed syllable transforms into the hand emblem, the bardo consciousness that has entered the union of seed and blood at the moment of conception is purified. The light then radiates and reabsorbs, and the hand emblem melts into light, corresponding to the development of the egg. The appearance of the deity corresponds to the moment the egg cracks open and the being is born.

Birth through heat and moisture is purified in a similar way. The sun disc represents heat, and the moon disc represents moisture. The seed syllable and hand emblem represent the bardo consciousness mixed with vital air. The radiation and reabsorption of the light and its transformation into the deity corresponds to the process of the consciousness entering the fusion of heat and moisture and being born.

Miraculous rebirth is purified in the following way: the seat of the deity is the birthplace of the bardo consciousness. The seed syllable and hand emblem represent the consciousness mixed with vital air. The light radiating and reabsorbing represents the consciousness' desire to take rebirth. It creates the power which nourishes the karmic potency to take rebirth in one instant—the way in which a miraculous rebirth occurs. The moment the deity appears is the moment of miraculous birth.

The process of the seed syllable's descent to the seat of the deity is called the sadhana of the syllables of speech. Every sadhana will have a hand emblem, a seed syllable or both. From either the hand emblem, the seed syllable or both, light radiates boundlessly into all directions in the form of offerings. The light invokes the pure intention awareness of all the buddhas and bodhisattvas and gathers blessings that then return and dissolve into the seed syllable. This is called the sadhana of the symbols of mind. Immediately thereafter, the hand emblem and/or seed syllable transforms into the complete form of the deity. Developing the complete form of the deity, with all the major and minor marks, is called the sadhana of the fully accomplished form.

This has been a general teaching on the sadhana of the fully accomplished form of the deity, as taught according to the generation stage. However, each sadhana is different. There are a great many distinctions regarding the characteristics of the deities, depending on whether they are peaceful or wrathful, Nirmanakaya, Sambhogakaya or Dharmakaya.

As the result of this practice, one gains the ability to take intentional rebirth in samsaric realms as a manifestation being of enlightened awareness to tame sentient beings. One gains the ability to determine where and from whom one will be born, so as to perform miraculous deeds for the welfare of others. Shakyamuni Buddha is a perfect example of one who achieved this result. He lived a life marked by the twelve miraculous deeds. This is the kind of result that comes by doing the practice and performing the stages of purification.

We will now consider the inner meaning of the hand emblems that the deities hold. Since there are many different kinds of hand emblems, we will consider only a few of the most common ones.

The five-pointed vajra, with four horns and a central shaft meeting at a point on each end, symbolizes the five primordial wisdoms. A nine-pointed vajra symbolizes the nine vehicles. The curved vajra knife symbolizes wisdom that severs discursive thoughts. A sword, like Manjushri's sword of wisdom, has more or less the same meaning as the trigug.

The skull cup is the vessel for bliss and primordial wisdom, symbolizing the state of being beyond the circle of discursive thought patterns. A skull cup filled with blood symbolizes the four negative forces, or the mind of samsara, which have been subdued by the greatness of primordial wisdom. It would be a mistake to think that the blood belonged to a demon slain by the deity who then drinks the blood with a victorious attitude. The deity does not have an attitude of desire or hatred. Properly understood, the blood represents the qualities of mercy and compassion, not hatred and desire. Of the two enlightened qualities, method and wisdom, the skull cup relates specifically to the wisdom quality.

The sword of wisdom also symbolizes cutting birth and death from the root. If you are not born, you will not die. The trident symbolizes severing the three poisons at their root. Everything about the deity's form is significant, and even though a deity may have many hands which hold many emblems, each of them has a specific inner meaning.

One face symbolizes the one form of the Dharmakaya. "One drop" means that all aspects are condensed into one single nature, absolutely supreme. Three heads (and faces) represent the three doors to liberation and the three kayas. Two hands symbolize the method of great mercy and the wisdom of emptiness. Four hands symbolize the four immeasurables—love, mercy, joy and equanimity. Six hands symbolize the five wisdoms and the naturally arising primordial wisdom. The adamantine posture, the *vajra asana*, symbolizes the equality of samsara and nirvana, the state of mind beyond the two extremes.

The nine characteristics of a peaceful deity express the deity's attractive appearance. These characteristics give one a comfortable feeling and prepare the mind for understanding peaceful qualities. The nine characteristics are: (1) soft, supple flesh to symbolize a pure birth; (2) perfectly proportioned and pliant body parts to symbolize purification of sickness and disease; (3) youthfulness, without any physical looseness, to symbolize purification of death; (4) a smooth appearance to symbolize purification of old age; (5) a form which appears like a perfectly endowed flower with a clean, clear complexion to symbolize possessing all pure qualities; (6) a beautiful, radiant form to symbolize purification of the sense fields; (7) an extremely attractive form for the purpose of taming beings; (8) a brilliant form to suppress negativity; and (9) splendor and blessing of the body which are the signs of vanquishing all things.

The deity's garments symbolize liberation from the suffering of delusion. An upper garment made from white silk with gold patterns on it, a lower garment made of various colors, and long, flowing scarves are examples of various garments the deities wear. Hair tied in a knot at the crown symbolizes having completed all virtuous dharmas. The jewels and flower ornaments symbolize carrying the energy of desire on the path to primordial wisdom, because the energy of desire is not rejected.

The jeweled ornaments symbolize the seven branches of the path of bodhicitta. The long necklace symbolizes mindfulness, the first branch. The crown symbolizes the investigation of the scriptures, the second branch. The bangles symbolize perseverance, the third branch. The earrings symbolize sublime purification, the fourth branch. Armlets symbolize perfected thought, the fifth branch. The medium-length necklace symbolizes equanimity, the sixth branch. The long, flowered rosary symbolizes joy, the seventh branch.

The characteristics of wrathful deities are as follows: three eyes symbolize omniscient knowledge of the three times—past, present and future—which can be seen simultaneously; four long fangs symbolize cutting at the root the four types of birth in cyclic existence; the wrathful deities' rough disposition, which mirrors one's own rough, gross appearance, is compassionately adopted to relate skillfully with one's ordinary disposition. A parent sometimes finds it necessary to scold a child, perhaps even harshly. Proper scolding is an expression of compassion and love which is meant to help the child, based on the knowledge that it is required to achieve the right effect. Some sentient beings are very difficult to tame with peaceful, expansive or powerful methods. Only a wrathful method can tame angry, disturbed, gross states of mind. The deity's wrath is really just an expression of intense compassion.

The nine gestures of the wrathful deities symbolize their embodiment of the five buddha families and the four consorts. These nine gestures are: (1) sensual and flirtatious, (2) heroic and brave, (3) disagreeable and disgusting, (4) wild and savage, (5) uttering strange sounds like "ha, ha" and "hee, hee" and making wrathful cries, (6) extremely wrathful and terrifying, (7) merciful, (8) threatening with gathering fury, and (9) peaceful.

The last characteristic is peaceful because ultimately the wrathful deity rests in a state of perfect peace and quiescence. The other gestures are simply expressions of the deity's fundamentally serene character. The nine characteristics of the peaceful deity are similar to those of the wrathful deity. Both peaceful and wrathful characteristics derive from the same source and perform the same symbolic function.

Continuing with the wrathful symbolism, the upper garment made of elephant skin symbolizes the ten strengths that subdue all delusion. The lower garment, the skirt made of tiger skin, symbolizes the courageous activity which subdues anger. The long, flowing silk scarf symbolizes the bodhicitta that subdues desire. The crown made of five dried skulls symbolizes pride subdued by receiving the qualities of the five buddhas. The long rosary made of fifty-one freshly cut human heads symbolizes subduing jealousy, paranoia and the fifty-one secondary minds that cause gross delusions to arise. The six bone ornaments and the six natural mudras symbolize the six perfections. The blazing five-colored fire of primordial wisdom surrounding the deities symbolizes the wisdom that comprehends selflessness, wisdom that can consume the three realms of cyclic existence.

Every deity has a supporting mandala of other deities, but before we discuss the deity's entourage, remember that the Nirmanakaya has the capacity to manifest in any form. Whatever is needed to tame sentient beings will manifest. The members of the entourage should be seen as manifestations or projections of the central deity. The members of the entourage arise from the central deity like rays of sunlight arise from the sun and are but one nature.

One should carry this way of thinking into one's approach to the four lineages or traditions in Vajrayana Buddhism— Nyingma, Kagyu, Sakya and Gelug. One should see the different heads of the lineages and their entourages the same way that one sees the deity and his entourage. For example, H.H. the Dalai Lama should be considered to be the central deity, and his entourage—his secretary, translator, servants, cooks, etc.—should be considered emanations from his form of enlightened awareness, like rays from the sun. The same is true concerning H.H. the Karmapa and the heads of the other lineages as well. In this way, you can exercise your faculty of pure perception.

Why is it necessary to develop pure perception? Because you have not recognized that you are the primordial Buddha. You have not realized that this lack of awareness is the only difference between yourselves and the primordial Buddha. You have not recognized that you have wandered in a state of cyclic confusion for countless lifetimes. If you constantly judge the guru's actions and those of everyone else, thinking that the guru is not the Buddha, you will never believe that you are the Buddha, and you will never achieve liberation. The technique which is most accepted as the one which will lead you to understand your perfect, true nature is the practice of pure perception, especially concerning your own guru.

It is most appropriate to practice pure perception toward the heads of the four lineages, all of whom fully realized their true nature long ago. They have been actively working for the sake of living beings for countless lifetimes.

This is another reason why it is extremely important to do the generation stage practices. The principal reason for the generation stage practices is to cut through ordinary mind and appearances. This is accomplished by generating the deity's mandala, practicing guru yoga, and by trying to practice pure perception in daily life as well.

You should also practice pure perception while visualizing the mandala. The mandala includes the celestial mansion, the seat of the principal deity and the deity's entourage. If you practice the generation stage with pure perception, you will realize the great, all-encompassing expanse of samsara and nirvana. You will realize that all appearance is the display of primordial wisdom. You will more easily realize this if you visualize that all phenomena, such as the mandala, arise from a single source.

The celestial mansion, deity and entourage are the unceasing display of primordial wisdom. Primordial wisdom, which is bliss and emptiness united, shows its illusory nature in the form of the deity's mandala. This play of truth is the only concept you should have about these appearances. You should never think that the deity and mandala have some origin other than wisdom, and you should never consider that this visualization has true inherent existence.

When you receive the teachings of the oral transmission directly introducing you to the nature of your mind (rigpa), you will know that the mind's nature is all-pervasive emptiness, that appearances are the natural display, and that unobstructed compassion is the energy quality. Rigpa meditation is the same as this generation stage practice of seeing all of the mandala's aspects arising from the central deity. The generation stage practice facilitates realization of the nature of one's mind.

When you create a display of your own primordial wisdom (which is why you visualize the deity and mandala), visualize it very purely, like a rainbow appearing, or like a star's reflection in a lake on a very clear night. You should realize that although the reflection of the star is not the actual star, it appears nevertheless with great clarity and precision. Your visualization should not be limited by concepts derived from your usual way of relating to the elements through your sense fields.

Conceive the entire mandala, including the different colors, hand emblems and other details having arisen from the main deity, in a manner similar to the multiplication of an image in a set of mirrors. In the visualization, all aspects of the mandala reflect off of the main deity. This is the explanation of how buddhas and bodhisattvas manifest from one source.

When you visualize, do not get hung up on details, do not approach visualization with an uptight mind. Instead, first build the visualization in a general way, and then, when it is complete, instead of going over details, be aware of the interdependence of the central deity and the mandala in the way just taught. This is very important for beginners because your minds have not relaxed into the nature of your own pure creativity. You lack the ability to clearly, instantaneously visualize the deity's form. It will aid your power to visualize if you develop strong awareness that all states of enlightened awareness originate from the Dharmakaya. The Dharmakaya is inconceivable, and it possesses unequalled qualities such as compassion and miraculous activities.

If all that has been taught so far—the visualization, the meaning of the symbols and the objects of purification, and so on—is a little overwhelming for a beginner, then just remember the overall beauty of the practice and how excellent the method is. Develop single-pointed fervent regard while you practice, and that should be sufficient. This will put your mind in the state where merit will be accumulated.

Meditating in this way will actually purify the processes of growth in the womb, and maturing through youth, adulthood and old age. It purifies the growth of desires and attachments such as wanting and needing to create and establish a worldly life made up of marriage, professional and social success, material wealth and so forth.

The meditation practice results in the achievement of the Nirmanakaya aspect of buddhahood and results in birth as an enlightened being. The Nirmanakaya is the manifestation being of enlightened awareness. You will gain the ability to work for the benefit of others and to fulfill compassionate purposes, by taking ordination and other vows and by practicing various difficult ascetic techniques and other positive activities. Giving up personal desires, you work for the welfare of others. Later on in life, as your exalted being matures, the essence of the awakened mind ripens, and fortunate disciples can reap the fruit. At such a stage of unfoldment, all negative states of mind are tamed and meditative concentration is achieved. You experience the taste of the ambrosial nectar of enlightenment and all omniscient qualities.

Finally, bless your body, speech and mind with the three vajra syllables. The three vajra syllables in your three places symbolize the intrinsic, absolute purity of the three doors of body, speech and mind. If you cannot accurately visualize the face, hands and other parts of the deity, then focus on the three vajra syllables in your three centers, effecting the mudra of the vajra syllables. By focusing in this way you will actualize the three vajra states of being—vajra body, speech and mind. This is an inconceivable experience.

Invoking the Primordial Wisdom Being and Requesting Stability

The state of primordial wisdom means having complete knowledge of all that is conventionally and ultimately true. To understand the ultimate, true nature of appearances, while simultaneously perceiving every conventionally existing karmic detail, is to experience the twofold mind of perfect wisdom, which is a mind free of limitation.

In the next section of the sadhana, you invoke the consecration of the primordial wisdom being (Tib. *ye shes sems dpa'*, pronounced "yeshe sempa"), into self-nature as the commitment being (Tib. *dam tshig sems dpa'*, pronounced "damtsig sempa"). Invoke the jnanasattva and ask him to remain. In the context of this invocation, the habits derived from environment, companions and intellectual development are the objects to be purified; the invocation of the wisdom beings with the request that they remain firm is the means of purification. The realization of the indivisible unity of intention of all enlightened beings is the result of purification.

The objects to purify are the habits that result from our environment, companions and intellectual development. From infancy to adulthood, each person spends much time acquiring various intellectual trainings, learning many things about his environment and culture. From these experiences, secondary habits and karmic instincts are developed, distinct from the primary instincts that already existed.

This is not to say that the qualities a person achieves in this lifetime are wrong. It is not the qualities that are poison. The problem is the way the mind relates with attachment to these qualities. Because the mind is deceived by these qualities and all the environmental and intellectual input, the attachment needs to be purified.

The practice that purifies the object is invoking the primordial wisdom being. From the HUNG in your heart, light radiates in the shape of hooks. The light draws the primordial wisdom beings from the naturally accomplished pure land. This pure land is not a created place, like the mandala you are creating; it is spontaneously accomplished, permeates all aspects of existence and is the resting place for primordial wisdom. The light radiates into this pure place and hooks all the pure wisdom energy. Do not think the hooking light has attachment. Think instead that the hooks represent your faith and devotion which draw in blessings.

The light is very white and radiant. As the light radiates from the HUNG in your heart, be aware of the richness and radiance of the HUNG. The light travels very swiftly and is empty in nature. It radiates into the ten directions (the eight cardinal points, above and below) and the four times (past, present, future and originally pure timeless time) and touches beings who have passed beyond all states of confusion and rest in the Dharmakaya. The invocation of light causes the Dharmakaya to stir and to arise as the Rupakaya, the form being of enlightened awareness. Countless aspects of your particular visualization, including the other deities in your mandala, the ornaments, garments, hand emblems and so forth, come forward in the space in front. Repeat the verses of invocation while you perform this visualization.

Exact replicas of your own visualized mandala pour down like falling rain from the ten directions, consecrating your meditational practice. Like water pouring into water, the primordial wisdom beings dissolve completely into the commitment beings, eliminating all distinction between the two. They become non-dual. Feel certain that the wisdom beings have taken their place within your mandala and then recite DZA HUNG BAM HO (see Plate III). This is recited in almost all sadhanas to confirm the invocation.

When you say DZA and form the proper mudra with your fingers, the commitment being hooks and draws forth the primordial wisdom beings. When you say HUNG and perform the mudra, the primordial wisdom and commitment beings merge, becoming non-dual. Reciting BAM confirms that the wisdom beings will remain until you accomplish whatever you want to accomplish, like attaining enlightenment or accomplishing the concerned activities of peace, expanse, power or wrath. Reciting HO commits the primordial wisdom beings to be with you until your purpose is achieved (see Appendix II).

The result occurs at the time buddhahood is achieved, when you realize that there is no distinction between Buddha and any other being who has passed beyond the wheel of confusion. You realize that all enlightened beings are indivisibly one in their pure enlightened intentionality.

Homage, Offering and Praise

After invoking the wisdom beings, your commitment mandala is now one with primordial wisdom. Realizing the full potential of this union, pay homage, make offerings and render praise. Here again there is an object to purify, the process of purification and the result. The objects to purify are the karmic instincts concerning the desire you have for wealth, family, fame and so forth. The practices which purify the object are homage, offering and praise.

The essential and ultimate achievement of Vajrayana meditation is to experience your own nature as identical with the form of the deity—the indivisible state of great bliss and emptiness, the state of primordial wisdom. When this time comes, the vital air and mind of great bliss arise as the form of the deity, the supreme mudra. This attainment fulfills the greatest spiritual desire, and those who achieve it can effortlessly perform any type of activity necessary to benefit sentient beings. They also possess the ability to rest in the mudra of union. By relying on this method, they swiftly achieve the ultimate result: the spontaneously born primordial wisdom. This is the ultimate meaning of homage. To cultivate proper respect, however, and to accumulate merit, visualize that replicas of your ordinary body emanate from your heart to pay homage to the indivisible nature of the sphere of emptiness and primordial wisdom. Imagining in this way, recite the verses of your particular sadhana. When you practice, you can accumulate great merit by recollecting the deity's different enlightened qualities as you pay homage. Recollect why the deity has, for example, one face, two arms and so forth.

Although the meditator recites verses of homage addressed to the deities, homage is actually directed to the ultimate nature of the mind in its twofold aspect of emptiness and primordial wisdom awareness. The true nature of the mind is obscured by the dual mind which constantly clings to the subject and grasps objects, thus creating the causes from which all other states of confusion and unhappiness arise. Because this dualistic attitude already exists, we set up another kind of dualistic situation in our meditation. Oneself appears as the meditator, the commitment beings appear from the force of the visualization, and the primordial wisdom beings appear from original purity. The commitment being and commitment mandala represent the sphere of emptiness; the primordial wisdom beings that are visualized merging into the commitment mandala represent the wisdom of emptiness. By recollecting the pure meaning of the symbols used in this practice, you are brought to the essential point which is the pure nature of the mind. Then you become able to render homage to the actual nature of the self.

Ultimately speaking, there is no person who meditates. No one invokes a separate entity to come and merge because only one nature exists to begin with. All that exists is the nature of wisdom mind, rigpa or pure awareness, and the expression of that awareness as it displays itself as variegated appearances. Ultimately speaking, invoking primordial wisdom brings you one step closer to the ultimate nature. After that step is taken, you can directly recognize your ultimate nature and pay homage accordingly.

Next is the practice of offering. There are four kinds of offerings: outer, inner, secret and actual nature. The outer "ordinary" offerings are accomplished in the following way. Visualizing yourself as the deity, from the center of your heart countless offering goddesses emanate. Each goddess holds in her hands one of the various objects that please the sense fields internally and externally. Innumerable goddesses emanate, filling the heavens with incomprehensible splendor. They then turn around to make their offerings directly to the deity. Recite the verses of your sadhana and effect this visualization. Feel that all the deities in your mandala receive the outer and inner offerings through their senses. The offerings enter the deities' corresponding sense organs (i.e. sound enters the ear, flavor enters the mouth, light enters the eyes, etc.) and come into their consciousnesses, bringing the entire experience from outside to inside. They thereby gain complete satisfaction.

The seven or eight offering bowls on the altar are an outer offering. When you offer them, visualize numberless offerings filling all of space. Even bowls that contain only water symbolize the seven traditional offerings.

The first bowl is the offering of pure, sweet, cool water for drinking (Tib. *mchod yon*, Skt. *argham*). The second bowl is the offering of very clear water for washing the feet (Tib. *shabs bsil*, Skt. *pādyam*). The third bowl, with flowers in it, is the offering of wonderfully beautiful flowers, made to crown the head (Tib. *me tog*, Skt. *puṣpe*). The fourth bowl contains incense made from flowers, musk, sandalwood or any natural substance (Tib. *bdug spos*, Skt. *dhūpe*). It is offered to the sense of smell. The fifth bowl is the offering of light (Tib. *mar me*, Skt. *āloke*) which is made to the eyes. It resembles a wish-fulfilling jewel able to illuminate the world with its brilliance. The sun and moon are natural sources of light in this world, but any source of light—lamps, candles, electric light—is an offering of light. The sixth offering of perfume (Tib. *dri chab*, Skt. *gandhe*) is made to the heart. The seventh offering is celestial food which can satisfy all gustatory desires with a single taste (Tib. *shal ze*, Skt. *naivedye*). This offering of perfect food is made to the tongue. The eighth offering is music from cymbals, wind instruments, drums, bells or any instrument that produces sounds that please the mind. (Tib. *rol mo*, Skt. *śabda*). This music is offered to the ears.

The countless offering goddesses surround you, holding these different outer and inner offerings. Imagine that, when they offer the flowers, the flowers dissolve into your crown causing you to experience inner satisfaction and sensual delight. The light dissolves into your eyes and the sound into your ears, which likewise delights these sense fields. This practice of offering is done solely for the sake of accumulating merit. The deity has no desires and does not seek to be fulfilled in this way. It would be a mistake to think otherwise. This completes our discussion of the outer offerings (see Plate IV).

The inner offerings are *men*, torma and rakta. All things, all dharmas in samsara and nirvana, are self-created. The actual nature of these dharmas is like pure nectar. The dharmas are not our individual creations. They are self-created, self-born. From the beginningless beginning, all dharmas have been in a state of original purity. Recognizing this is making the offering of *men*, medicine. On the altar, the *men* offering is placed in the skull cup to the right of the central torma.

There are one thousand different types of medicines made from a combination of leaves, branches, twigs, etc., everyone of them possessing this pure nature. The term "elixir" or "medicine" describes all the different sacred materials that have the power of healing. Since all dharmas in samsara and nirvana have an originally pure nature, it cannot truthfully be said that one thing is medicine and another is not. Since all materials are equal as far as their true nature is concerned, separate yourself from the dualistic mind which labels and forms discursive thoughts. Separating yourself from this negative mind causes every material thing to become a source of healing: medicine. Ultimately, all materials are medicine when you see their true, original state of purity, once you discard the attitude of mind that conceives of them as being impure. So when making the offering of medicine, have an awareness of the equality of all substances.

To perform the offering of medicine, use the skull cup on the table in front of you that contains a little nectar and perhaps some blessing pills or other substance that has been blessed. Take your ring finger and thumb and press them together to symbolize the union of sun and moon, of samsara and nirvana. Dip these fingers into the skull cup's contents and sprinkle a few drops. The drops multiply without limit and dissolve into the mouths of all the enlightened beings who are gathered, causing them to experience the wisdom of bliss and emptiness. All these beings become satisfied. This is the offering of *men*.

Next, the meditator offers the torma. The torma offering is symbolic of the dharmadhatu, the sphere of ultimate truth. The dharmadhatu/torma offering is measureless, like a sphere without beginning or end. It is composed of unequalled substances: food, drink and all substances that sentient beings desire and which please the sense fields. These food and drink offerings possess the nature of primordial wisdom.

To offer the torma, recite the verses in your sadhana and visualize each deity to be endowed with a tongue shaped like a vajra with a hollow, reed-like spine. As the deities extract the essence of the torma through the hollow centers of their vajra tongues, their hearts become extremely pleased. The ultimate meaning of this visualization is that the deities are extracting the essence of the object and its consciousness, transforming everything into the expanse of clear light awareness. They are not delighting in the actual food and drink but in this state of awareness.

To offer the rakta, consider that the root of suffering is compulsory attachment condensed together as the rakta. Dissolving into the expanse of desireless great bliss, samsara is set free in the unborn sphere of truth. This precious substance, the rakta, is then offered to the gathered assembly of deities in the mandala. The vast ocean of samsara's blood is instantly partaken of without leaving any remainder.

This has been a very brief explanation of the outer and inner offerings. We proceed now to a brief explanation of the secret offerings. There are two types of secret offering: the offering of union and the offering of liberation. In the offering of union, one perceives the union of male and female principles of enlightened awareness by considering all appearances to be the natural expression of the male principle of enlightened awareness and by considering that the empty, wisdom nature of the object is the female principle of enlightened awareness. These two—the appearance and its empty nature—are indivisibly one from the beginningless beginning. The nature of appearance is emptiness, and the expression of emptiness is appearance. The fact that these two are indivisible is expressed through the secret offering of union.

The practices found in anuyoga are another expression of the secret offering. In the *tsa lung* practices of anuyoga, the meditator works with the inner psychic body, the channels, the energies and the practice of union to taste the great bliss. In this practice, all the deities residing in the different channels within the practitioner's body become fully satisfied when they taste the experience of simultaneous bliss and emptiness. In the generation stage practices, as in all inner practices, the deities are depicted in union with consort. This is called yab yum. Yab is the male principle, the natural expression of appearance, and yum is the female principle, the natural empty wisdom nature of appearance. The actual offering of union, from a secret point of view, occurs when the deities' secret centers are joined. The secret offering is always expressed by this union.

Even solitary deities incorporate the yab yum symbolism, though in a different fashion. The presence of the secret consort of a solitary deity may be symbolized by a trident held by the deity, or by the appearance of a tiny buddha, representing the head of the family to which the particular deity belongs, projecting from the deity's crown.

A practitioner of dzog rim, the completion stage, will visualize his/her own form as the deity while engaging in practices that involve moving the energy up and down through the channels where the different experiences of bliss are achieved, moving the energy between the visualized bodies of the two deities. These practices are performed to experience great bliss, and when practicing them it is very important to always hold the pride of the deity and maintain awareness of the secret offering.

It is not exactly clear how Westerners got the idea that married couples, or, for that matter, any couple having a lot of desire for each other, could practice the Vajrayana techniques taken from tantric Buddhism or some other spiritual tradition. They try to visualize themselves as deities but then engage in an ordinary sexual act based on attachment/desire. They want an experience of something more blissful than ever before. This is one of the biggest mistakes a person can make. This activity does not even approximate the practices we are discussing. One who attempts tantric practices in this way, lacking the proper prerequisites and permission from the vajra guru, just accumulates causes for lower rebirth—even, perhaps, causes for the lowest possible rebirth, since this is to misuse and disrespect pure Dharma practice. Pure Dharma has nothing to do with ordinary sexual desire.

Since deities do not have desires, it is a grave error to visualize oneself as a deity to achieve purposes conceived by a desiring mind. When an anuyoga tsa lung practitioner becomes adept, gaining complete control over his or her channels, winds and essential fluids, he or she can perform extremely profound practices. A yogi or yogini who practices with a partner must not lose even one drop of essential fluid and must definitely be free of desire or attachment. To perform these secret practices, a practitioner must be on a very high level and must practice solely for the sake of sentient beings. When a practitioner arrives at this level of practice, it is very wonderful, but one must wait until the right time arrives.

The practices of union are the most secret for a number of reasons. For instance, one will not even hear of and certainly will not receive a transmission for these practices from anyone but one's own guru, who can communicate them only through direct oral transmission. These practices are protected with secrecy because, of all desirable activities, human beings have the greatest desire for sex, and this desire causes them to misuse and misinterpret the practices. If human beings, motivated by sexual desire, attempt these most advanced techniques without being qualified, they will definitely suffer in lower rebirths. This is, in fact, one of the fastest ways to be born into the lower realms. These practices are kept secret to prevent their being misused.

You must understand that the Vajrayana practices are the swiftest of all Buddhist teachings and the most secret. They are protected ever so carefully by the protector deities (*dharmapalas*). If you misuse these practices, the dharmapalas create obstacles for you and your teachers. For instance, a potentially long life could be shortened. It is very important to refrain from running after teachers and receiving empowerments without first checking with your root teacher to see whether you are ready for them. Be very careful if you hear that some very secret empowerment is going to be given, because if you get involved with something for which you are unprepared, the repercussions could be very serious. It could even ruin your path.

The next offering is the secret offering of liberation. The object to be liberated is the view that a self truly exists. This view arises from the dualistic mind that grasps to subject and object and creates all discursive thoughts. This secret offering is meant to liberate the egocentric view.

Holding this view, sentient beings are thrown from one lifetime to another, through an endless series of rebirths in cyclic existence.

You need to absolutely annihilate this ego. Until you realize that non-dualistic mind truly exists and until you understand the true nature of the mind, this dualistic mind—big ego—is your worst enemy.

This dualistic mind is simply a consequence of not understanding the empty nature of appearances and the appearance nature of emptiness. At more advanced levels of spiritual realization, when you realize the nature of your mind, you will see subtle obscurations, as you now face gross obscurations. Right now you are preoccupied with gross obscurations and are unaware of the subtle ones. By recognizing the true nature of appearances, you gradually eliminate all gross obscurations. By recognizing the true nature of emptiness, you eliminate all subtle obscurations. Thus you are liberated.

Do you understand who the enemy is? You do not need to beat anyone up, and you do not need a weapon to kill your enemy. You do not need money to buy a weapon. It is all very easy.

How is liberation accomplished? The offering of liberation is accomplished by abandoning the dualistic mind of discursive thoughts. The sharp weapon of primordial wisdom, which completely annihilates the dualistic mind, is the means for achieving this separation. This "weapon" has been part of your continuum for a long time now. With this weapon you can completely devastate the dualistic mind, leaving not even a trace behind, thus liberating the mind into the sphere of unborn truth. The enemy will never return. This is called great liberation.

I must emphasize that primordial wisdom is not something you can buy, get from your best friend or have handed to you by a buddha in heaven. It is not something that someone else has but you do not. Abandon such concepts. Primordial wisdom does not come from an external source. It is simply your true nature. It is something that you and everyone else have as the very essence of your mind.

You should all know what your qualities and capabilities are. Don't you want to know what your highest qualities are? The unborn, primordial wisdom is the nature of your being from beginningless time. It is something you all possess as your innermost essence. It is like a flower within, like a bud that has not yet blossomed. It has not blossomed because you have not recognized its existence, and therefore have not given it the right light or provided the proper elements. This flower is not like the flowers painted on the altar, like the notes you are writing, or like the tapes you listen to after class. You rely on these manufactured dharmas to learn about and reflect on the true Dharma. The whole point of these practices is to make the flower blossom from within. You will never find the blossom outside yourself. Never!

It is very important to take notes, to listen, contemplate and meditate, but all the while remain aware that the essence is contained within. The search is simply to help you perceive your nature. When you see your nature for the first time, it will really be something to marvel at. It will astound you. It will be such an amazing discovery you just will not believe it. It is the greatest gift and has been within you all the time.

The term "yedrol chenpo" (Tib. *ye grol chen po*) means great, original liberation. This indicates the fact that our nature has always been liberated. In the Mahayana, the vehicle of cause and result, the Buddha taught that the buddha essence is possessed by all living creatures. But Vajrayana is a vehicle of result. Here, cause and result are identical; there is no distinction between them. This is why it is called the great original liberation. The belief in the existence of a self is liberated by perceiving the self's total lack of true, inherent existence. The self has not even one atomic particle worth of real substance. Since the self, the object to be liberated, has never attained true existence, the meditator perceives it as a mirage or an illusion. With this kind of understanding, the object can be liberated. All discursive thoughts are placed in the dharmadhatu, and the object is liberated into the equality of samsara and nirvana. This explains the secret offering of union and the offering of liberation.

The fourth type of offering is the absolute offering, or the offering of the nature as it is. To perform the absolute offering, you must enter into the awareness that all dharmas, all appearances in samsara and nirvana, are perfectly pure from the beginning. All appearances are the spontaneously accomplished great mandala of the Buddha. Remember that the word "mandala" does not refer exclusively to the multicolored drawings you have seen. In this context we are referring to the spontaneously accomplished mandala, the way things are, the natural state of appearance. This is the great mandala of the buddhas.

In this spontaneously accomplished mandala, the three concepts of offerer, offering and recipient must be understood to be empty in nature. Offering must be performed in a state of emptiness without conceptualization. Then it will be an absolute offering, of the nature as it is, the Great Seal or Mahamudra. This offering is unsurpassable. It is the most important and most powerful type of offering.

How do you make this offering? It is true that when you offer this way, there is nothing else to do. When you are in a state of pure awareness (rigpa), realizing the true nature of your mind, unsurpassable offering naturally occurs constantly with everything you perceive. But this is difficult for you now.

You should know that rigpa, the primordial wisdom nature which is the nature of the mind, has nothing to do with personality or the conceptual mind. It is the essential nature of each and every human being, without exception, never changing. This nature cannot be changed by the different forms, personalities and characteristics that a person assumes as a wanderer in cyclic existence. It cannot be changed because it is unborn and unceasing. It is the nature as it always has been and always will be. To the degree that you are unfamiliar with this understanding, you are unlikely to have recognized the original nature.

The secret offerings of union and liberation and the absolute offering are part of every sadhana, even though they may be indicated by only a word. Usually, they come after the outer and inner offerings. Even though the corresponding verses may be brief, meditate for some period of time on their meaning and importance. These four offerings sow the seeds that bear the fruit of the four kayas (Dharmakaya, Sambhogakaya, Nirmanakaya and Svabhavakaya).

The next portion of the practice is the act of rendering praise. Recollect the qualities and symbolism of the mandala, the seats of the deities, the deities, the hand emblems, the seed syllables and whether the deity is of the peaceful, expansive, powerful or wrathful class. Make praises with awareness of the deity's qualities and of the nature of the mind.

The deity acts effortlessly to assist sentient beings who have ripened karmic connections. This activity, which tames the minds of sentient beings, is spontaneously accomplished in a variety of ways simply by remembering the needs of sentient beings. Therefore, praises are made to the deity by recollecting all these enlightened qualities. To praise the deity's qualities is to praise the first of the three inner Vajrayana vehicles, the mahayoga. The deity's qualities are also represented by the nine vehicles, which are made available to benefit sentient beings. When all sentient beings achieve liberation and the ocean of cyclic existence is emptied, these nine vehicles will no longer be needed. They exist only because sentient beings need them.

Offering praises is extremely meaningful because it produces a highly positive result, unlike the worldly praise that you lavish on each other, which does not produce virtuous results. When offering praises, be aware that the object praised and the subject praising are indivisible and that the nature which is praised is identical with both subject and object. Absolute praise is the same as the absolute offering. Be aware that the object is empty and that the subject and activity are without true, inherent existence. Resting in a state of pure awareness, offer praise.

You will not be practitioners on the path forever. One day you will become realized and achieve the results. Therefore, it is important to be aware of the results arising from making offerings and praise. When you obtain enlightenment and become a buddha, you will not need to wish for anything ever again. You will, in fact, become the object of offering and veneration, and the experience of receiving boundless offerings will be your own waking reality. You will perceive only endless, unsurpassable offerings and praise, and this experience will pervade all of samsara and nirvana.

A liberated person will never experience fear or any problem concerning survival. He or she will always be taken care of. Such persons will always have a place to stay or will always receive offerings of food. They will not need to get jobs. They never even have to ask for things. People will simply make offerings out of love. It might seem like a miracle or a benefit gained by cleverness, but it is neither of these. It is exclusively the result of perfecting this practice.

Take for example the Pope, or any true religious leader who is an object of veneration. Wherever they go, people are very glad to take care of them. H.H. the Dalai Lama, H.H. Karmapa and H.H. Dudjom Rinpoche are good examples. Wherever they go, they are taken care of. For you, it may be difficult wherever you go.

This completes the sections on homage, offering and praise.

Training in the Visualization of the Principal Deity

We now begin the training in the visualization of the principal deity. The training involves four practices. First is the achievement of clarity concerning the deity's characteristics; second, the achievement of the stable pride of the deity; third, the development of pure recollection regarding the deity's pure qualities; and fourth, the training in the arising of bliss, clarity and emptiness. All four of these practices should be present while performing the deity yoga.

Unless you can spontaneously visualize the entire form of the deity with a single effort, it is best to generate it step by step. Generate the visualization gradually, from the bottom of the lotus feet to the top of the jeweled crown.

In the first session, spend most of your time clarifying the various parts of the lotus base and deity's seat. Then proceed to the deity's feet, legs and so on, clarifying each part before you go on to the next. Eventually, you will be able to visualize the entire form. Next, put the ornaments and garments on the deity from the head and going down to the feet.

In the beginning, the most important thing is to achieve clarity in your visualization. The goal of the meditator is to visualize the deity and all his characteristics as clearly as the moon is reflected in a crystal clear pond on a clear night, or as clearly as the peach fuzz on a face is reflected in a really excellent mirror. You need to be able to visualize every single aspect of the deity in clear, precise detail. The goal is that, at some point, you will be able to instantly arise as the deity as clearly as you now perceive your ordinary body.

It does not matter whether your eyes are open or closed. What matters is that your mind gains the ability to have a clear visualization that arises the instant you say the deity's name. When you accomplish this, when the deity appears suddenly, it is an excellent sign. To achieve this goal, recall the deity whenever you can, not only when you are sitting in meditation and practicing your sadhana. When you eat, just before you fall asleep, when you are walking, or any time you are not necessarily concentrating mentally on something, be aware of the visualization and continue to work on achieving clarity.

This practice obviously demands a tremendous amount of perseverance. You will never gain a clear visualization of any deity without applying an incredible amount of diligent effort to the practice.

The second practice is to gain the stable pride of the deity. Vajra pride is a different kind of pride from the poisonous pride that you have already firmly achieved. It is an expression of a state wherein all faults have been exhausted and all potential enlightened qualities have become actual. When you meditate on yourself as the deity, you are in fact meditating on your own true nature as represented by that form. Holding the pride of your buddha nature, represented by the enlightened form of the deity, gain a sense of stability. This pride should be with you constantly.

This vajra pride is very clear. It is not the poisoned pride of the ego. In your present deluded state, if someone calls your name, you immediately zero in on that sound with attachment because it concerns your ego. Be very mindful not to have this kind of concept when you are visualizing yourself as the deity. Keep your mind very clear and pure, and then you will be practicing the generation stage purely.

In the state of enlightened awareness, your own true nature, appearances and the empty nature of appearances exist. Although devoid of inherent existence, appearances arise as the illusory display, the playfulness of the empty nature. Appearance is the generation stage visualization and so is holding the stable pride of the deity. Maintaining awareness of the empty nature is the completion stage. The generation stage and completion stage are indivisibly united, just as appearance and emptiness are one true nature.

By holding the pride of the deity, you purify your ordinary, impure conceptions. These conceptions are impure because they obscure the true nature of appearances, causing you to cling to objects as truly existing. The mind of dualistic awareness causes you to perceive appearances as impure and ordinary. Holding the stable pride of the deity purifies this.

Purification is the practice of achieving clarity, practicing pure recollection of the deity's qualities and the symbolism of the deity's enlightened appearance, holding the stable pride of the deity, and training in the arising of bliss, clarity and emptiness. These practices help you to achieve perfect meditative concentration upon the deity.

The third step is to contemplate the deity's pure qualities by remembering the significance of the deity's attributes, such as the number of heads and limbs that it possesses. This is pure recollection.

As we have been saying all along, the essence of pure mind is primordial wisdom. From beginningless time the mind's nature has been Buddha, possessing boundless qualities. Most importantly, these qualities are natural, self-born and spontaneously accomplished.

There are two kinds of deities—wisdom deities and meditational deities. The meditational deity is visualized either in the space in front of you or as yourself. The wisdom deity, on the other hand, is a pure emanation of enlightened awareness; it has been pure from beginningless time and is not a mental recreation of a pure image. It might seem that by visualizing a meditational deity you are creating a pure form, but visualizing the deity is more than a creative act.

As you recite the verses in your sadhana that describe the deity's appearance, focus your awareness on the pure meaning of the various characteristics of the deity's appearance. Do not sit idly, reciting words without awareness.

When performing deity yoga, even if you are not able to effect a clear visualization, abandon doubts and impure concepts about the deity's form. At the very least, always maintain intense, fervent devotion towards the deity's pure form. While you work on developing a clear visualization, simultaneously contemplate the pure meaning of the deity's attributes.

The two practices—achieving clarity of visualization and practicing pure recollection—must always be performed simultaneously; enter a state of meditative concentration upon both. Without this, your visualization will either lack either meaning or clarity. Practicing with both, you will notice that deity pride is generated naturally.

The fourth practice is to train in the arising of bliss, clarity and emptiness. It is vital to remember that the three elements that are so important to the generation stage practice—clarity, pure recollection and stable pride—are empty in nature. Do not allow these three practices to become just another series of discursive thoughts.

It is also extremely important to accustom yourself to the view that, although its nature is empty, the deity's form appears naturally, in the same way that a reflection appears in water, or a rainbow appears in the sky. It appears yet has no inherent existence.

The best way to practice the generation stage is to seal every aspect of your visualization with the power of the completion stage. You do this by remaining aware that appearances are an expression of your empty nature. Sealing your visualization in this way will make your entire visualization a display of the Dharmakaya. This is the best way to practice.

Ordinarily when doing the generation stage practices, the intellect is used to visualize the mandala, thus accumulating ordinary merit. But as the deity and mandala are actually uncompounded since beginningless time, the intellect cannot touch any of the mandala's true aspect. Wisdom merit is accumulated when you practice with awareness of the empty nature. By thus sealing the generation with the completion stage, you simultaneously accumulate ordinary and wisdom merit.

As a result of accumulating the two types of merit, one realizes the two kayas (Dharmakaya and Rupakaya), the two truths (ultimate and conventional) and the indivisibility of wisdom and method. Therefore, Vajrayana, the secret Mantrayana, is called the swiftest, most profound vehicle. Many people believe that Vajrayana is something magical; Vajrayana is magical only if you know how to actualize its potential. Practicing in this way will create a swift, magical path for you.

It is important to understand this matter of the deity's pure, radiant, empty nature. If you simply visualize yourself as the deity, thinking that you are as real as a table, and remain unaware of the pure meaning of the deity's characteristics, you will not be following the Vajrayana path. Even if you gain an exquisite sense of clarity and stability in this visualization, your practice will not lead to enlightenment.

Someone who practices the generation stage while retaining a sense of selfhood will probably achieve a species of pride of the deity, but no true vajra pride. False deity pride is founded on the meditator's belief in the inherent existence of the deity with which he has become identified. This eternalistic belief binds a meditator to cyclic existence; it is a very heavy obscuration. A meditator who visualizes a peaceful deity and holds this mistaken view will experience rebirth as a god in the form realm. There are many accounts of practitioners who, holding such a view, visualized wrathful deities and were reborn as cannibals, demons or spirits. These accounts are recorded in many books on Mantrayana. Believing that a peaceful or wrathful deity actually exists is a delusion of the same nature as having a strong concept of self-identity. Thinking, "I really exist," and believing so strongly in this ego, you create great clinging.

Perform the generation stage practices of clear visualization, recollecting the pure qualities and gaining stability of deity pride in a pure manner and for as long as you are able. To achieve the results, practice in daily sessions and persevere through weariness. It is extremely important to persevere for long periods of time. Begin recitation of the mantra when you become weary of visualizing due to the intense effort you have expended.

CHAPTER V

The Actual Practice:
The Yoga of Meditative Equipoise
Part II

The Yoga of the Speech Recitation

The next section explains the yoga of vajra recitation in seven parts: (1) general understanding, (2) the particular necessity for practice, (3) the actual nature of the recitation, (4) different types of recitation, (5) the manner of reciting the mantra, (6) number of recitations and (7) activity upon completion.

General Understanding

A general understanding of the yoga of vajra recitation is approached by considering the object that needs to be purified by the yoga, the means of purification and the result. The object that needs to be purified through the yoga of speech is the habit of perceiving all sounds—names, words, syllables and anything that is spoken—as merely ordinary sounds with ordinary meanings.

Simply stated, the object to purify is your present, obscured experience of speech and the habitual instincts that accompany it. The practice of mantra recitation purifies this impure experience and results in pure, vajra-like speech. One achieves the Sambhogakaya and becomes imbued with the sixty qualities of the Buddha's speech. All of one's words become pleasing, meaningful and helpful. The means of purification is to recite the mantra, the pure sounds which the buddhas have given to us, over and over until they are like a spinning wheel of sound.

The result of this purification practice is the attainment of vajra speech. When you become enlightened, as you all will, your activity will be directed toward taming beings. Exercising the miraculous activity of vajra speech is called "turning the wheel of the Dharma." We work to attain vajra speech and its attendant powers to prepare for this auspicious time.

The Particular Necessity for Practice

The second part discusses "the particular necessity for practice." Through the power of the yoga of speech, the stains that obscure the mind are removed. Once this happens, speech reaches its full potential. It is like discovering the true nature of your speech for the very first time.

To activate the yoga of speech, summon the primordial wisdom deities by calling their names. Just as calling someone's name naturally causes that person to draw closer to you, in the same way calling the wisdom deities by name brings them nearer to you. They come to see what you want.

This does not mean the wisdom deities will not come if you do not call them. They could come even if you did not call their names. You call their names—which is what you are doing when you recite mantras—because their names express their actual nature. A quote from the *Dorje Kur (rDo rje gur)* scripture reads: "To directly perceive the buddhas, bodhisattvas, dakinis and your own consort, get their attention by calling their names and invite them to come." Reciting the deity's name over and over purifies obscurations of speech and establishes the cause of vajra speech.

This cause produces the condition that averts adverse conditions. The speech of the wisdom deities and your own speech will become the same—vajra speech.

The Actual Nature of Recitation

The third section discusses the manner of reciting mantras. Mantras arise due to the compassion of enlightened beings. To establish karmic connections and liberate beings in cyclic existence, enlightened beings residing in the sphere of ultimate, true awareness arise, in a manner of speaking, and manifest in various forms. However, in an ultimate sense, they do not stir from perfect equipoise. For the same purpose, the enlightened ones manifest sounds: speech, name syllables and audible expressions of every sort. Their speech manifests in the form of mantra syllables that, in fact, are their own names. In this way mantra syllables are transmitted to the conventional plane.

Mantra recitation should be practiced by repeating the syllables over and over for a long period of time. In this way you call the names of the wisdom deities of enlightened awareness. If you recollect the qualities of the deity while you recite the mantra and rest in a state of primordial wisdom, you will certainly attract the wisdom energy and make a connection that cannot fail.

Whenever you do vajra recitations and recite the names of the buddhas, you will always make a connection that will produce extremely powerful results. One of the temporal results that one may acquire is the ability to perform various activities that are beneficial to others through one's speech, using peaceful, powerful, wrathful or expansive methods. As the blessings and spiritual transmissions enter and purify your speech, their effect is to reveal the true nature of your speech, which was there all along. Ultimately, your speech actually becomes the enlightened speech of the buddhas. This is the true meaning of the nature of vajra recitation.

Your visualization practice must always be infused with three qualities: (1) clarity, (2) the stable pride of the deity and (3) pure recollection of the meaning of the visualization. Simultaneously, you must maintain a general, clear awareness of the empty and blissful nature of appearances. In this state of true visualization, meditate on the deity's precious heart, which should be visualized as a hollow, circular area, like the empty space inside a tent. This space has neither outer nor inner existence, yet it appears as a clear, translucent space devoid of any obscuration.

Within the deity's heart, clearly visualize a tiny seat formed of a solar and lunar disk. Then, according to your particular sadhana, visualize the jnanasattva, the pure wisdom being, seated thereon. The jnanasattva is a tiny replica of yourself as the deity seated in your heart. Although you are the meditational being, the samaya-sattva, at this point in the sadhana you have invoked the pure wisdom energy and possess the ability to radiate innumerable manifestations of yourself.

Consider the tiny wisdom being in your heart to be the Sambhogakaya aspect and consider yourself, as the major deity, to be the Nirmanakaya aspect. For example, if you are visualizing yourself as Avalokiteshvara, the wisdom being in your heart would always be Amitabha. If you visualize yourself as Yeshe Tsogyal, the wisdom being is always the Sambhogakaya dakini, Vajra Varahi—Dorje Phagmo. Each particular sadhana will specify who the Sambhogakaya deity will be.

Within the heart space of the wisdom being, there is another circular tent-like area. In that radiant space, clear and free of obscuration, visualize the hand emblem for your particular main deity. Each main deity belongs to one of the five buddha families, and each family is represented by a different hand emblem. Whether your particular practice emphasizes peace, power, expanse or wrath, a particular hand emblem appropriate to the deity's character will be prescribed by the sadhana. The hand emblem in the pure wisdom being's heart is visualized in a vertical position.

For example, a meditator who is generating a deity of the vajra family might visualize a nine-pointed vajra in the wisdom being's heart. It would be an error to conceive it as a solid, material vajra. A vajra is the weapon of primordial wisdom and should be visualized by the meditator as translucent and devoid of tangible substance, similar to a rainbow.

In the hollow center of the hand emblem, the meditator will visualize a solar or lunar disk seat. Atop the solar or lunar seat visualize the *samadhisattva*, the single-pointed concentration being. The samadhisattva is the seed syllable of life, the very essence of the deity. This syllable could be HUNG or HRI. Visualize it very clearly, like a candle flame. It stands vertically, facing in the same direction as the deity in whose heart it appears. If the deity faces east, then the syllable faces east. It possesses the same brilliant color as the deity and shines radiantly.

To summarize, then: first, the meditator visualizes himself or herself as the meditational being; second, he or she visualizes the pure wisdom being in his or her heart; and third, in the heart of the wisdom being he or she visualizes the single-pointed concentration being.

This is the sequence for visualizing the three sattvas. Some sadhanas, however, do not incorporate visualization of all three beings. More common and extensive practices include all three sattvas; but shorter practices, for whatever reason, sometimes omit the pure wisdom being or the hand emblem. In any event, all sadhanas direct the meditator to visualize himself or herself as the meditational being, with the seed syllable in his or her heart.

The letters of the mantra encircle the central syllable. The first syllable of the mantra is visualized in front of the seed syllable in the deity's heart. Visualize the mantra's syllables to be extremely fine, as if each had been drawn with a brush made of a single hair. The syllables are very precise, each appearing in its own place without touching the other.

You can visualize the mantric syllables in whatever script you are most familiar with; they do not necessarily have to be written in the Tibetan or Sanskrit script. However, it is important to try to visualize them in the Tibetan script since it has been used for such a long time by the great realized ones. To do so will sow auspicious seeds. Later you can visualize them in whatever script you are most familiar with and try it that way. If you begin this way, it will be very easy to relate to the Tibetan.

Actually, the language you have spoken your entire life has already caused the channels and knots throughout your body and entire psychic being to take on the shapes and forms of the syllables of your native language. This is why it is acceptable to visualize mantras in your native language; your channels are already completely formed with the nature of those syllables.

Still, it is better to recite the mantras in Sanskrit. For example, it would be very strange to recite the English translation of the mantra OM AH HUNG VAJRA GURU PEMA SIDDHI HUNG. It would become so wordy. Think about trying to say the One-Hundred-Syllable mantra of Vajrasattva in English simultaneously trying to visualize all the English syllables going around. This would be quite difficult. Therefore, try and learn the Sanskrit sounds of the mantras.

The main purpose of practicing mantrayana, mantra recitation, is not to visualize the syllables or hear their sounds. The main purpose is to induce the spiritual transmission to enter the mind of the practitioner who has faith and fervent regard towards the meaning of the practice. Sounds and syllables are merely mental supports. To receive the blessings that lead one to realize the ultimate, true nature as it is, a practitioner must focus his or her mind on the meaning of the pure characteristics and qualities of the visualization. If you have a lot of faith, are aware of the meaning, and recite the syllables and sounds as correctly as possible, then you will certainly receive blessings from vajra recitation, due simply to your understanding of the essential meaning of the practices.

Different Types of Recitation

The fourth section discusses the four ways in which mantras are visualized: first, the placement of mantric syllables and the reasons for that placement; second, the type of mantra that is likened to a comet in space or to a sparkler making a trail; third, the type of mantra that is likened to a king's messenger; and fourth, the type of mantra that is likened to a beehive.

Fundamentally, it is most important to rely upon your particular sadhana. Be clearly aware of how many mantras encircle the seed syllable—sometimes there are two or three. You must know whether the sadhana is brief or extensive.

All mantras are led by the syllable OM and are concluded by a syllable such as HUNG or HRI. During recitation a mantra is visualized encircling the seed syllable. If the mantra turns in a clockwise direction, then the syllables, beginning with the first and continuing in sequence, will be lined up in a counterclockwise direction facing toward the seed syllable which they surround. If the mantra turns in a counterclockwise direction, then the syllables are lined up going clockwise. Each syllable should be visualized clearly and distinctly, standing upright in its own place.

A mantra is visualized as a closed loop, without gaps. In a long mantra, like the One-Hundred-Syllable mantra, the syllable OM and the ending syllable AH always occupy the places directly in front of the seed syllable. The entire effect is very symmetrical.

Generally speaking, the mantras of male deities, representing skillful means, circle clockwise. The mantras of female deities, representing wisdom, usually circle counterclockwise. But these things occasionally differ, so refer to the sadhana's commentary.

Practices which are performed to extend the guru's life, or any other practice which protects the lama, are enhanced by visualizing the seed syllable and the guru as indivisible. Visualize your guru seated in the hollow space described by the shape of the seed syllable. You can visualize other suffering sentient beings in this place also. When performing a long-life blessing to extend a person's life, visualize their life essence contained within the syllables AH and NRI (see Appendix II).

The first practical step in visualizing the seed syllable and mantra is to gain clarity in visualizing the seed syllable. Second, work on the mantra until you know what each syllable is and how each is placed in relation to the others. Third, work on clearly visualizing the spinning mantra. Eventually, it just spins on its own without any kind of mental effort, the syllables floating frictionlessly above the seat which is below them. Visualize them floating in this way as they rotate around the seed syllable.

The second type of mantra glows like a whirling sparkler or a ring of fire, expressing the enlightened activity of power. It is accomplished in the following way. From the light of the original mantra, which has been circling rapidly, a second mantra emanates and encircles the first mantra. The two mantras barely touch each other. They look like two concentric rings.

This second ring of the two-ringed mantra leaves the mouth of the pure wisdom being (jnanasattva) and then flows out of the mouth of the meditational being (samayasattva) to enter the mouth of the consort, the yum. It proceeds down through her central channel and into her lotus or secret center. It reenters the body of the yab through his secret vajra and rises to reenter his heart, forming a circular chain of mantric syllables. The mantra dissolves, one syllable at a time, into the corresponding seed syllable of the mantra that has remained turning in the heart. The syllables then re-emerge to circle again through the body of the yum and back into the yab. As this pattern continues, it resembles a ring of fire. The male and female deity experience intense inexhaustible bliss that is indivisible with emptiness—they experience the actual nature of bodhicitta. "Male deity" and "female deity" refer only to the meditator who is visualizing self-nature as a pair of deities in union. As each syllable dissolves, the meditator experiences the great bliss of primordial wisdom and receives the supreme spiritual attainment. If a meditator has generated the self-form as the deity and generated another deity in the space in front, this type of recitation may also be performed between the two of them.

Many temporal powers are attained through this practice: one's life span increases, pure qualities become fully endowed, the wisdom nature unfolds, and one becomes well known as a spiritual being and gains various spiritual abilities that can be used to assist others.

Do you understand all of this? It is good to think about these teachings repeatedly, since they are difficult to understand after only a single hearing. If you do not study the teachings, nothing much will come from your simply hearing them.

The third type of mantra practice is likened to the messenger of a king and is performed in the following way. The meditator visualizes light radiating from the rosary of syllables in his or her heart filling all of space with light of the color prescribed by the sadhana. This light bears offerings to the buddhas and enlightened ones, who also pervade space, pleasing their minds and hearts. The light then returns and redissolves into the self-visualized deity, enriching the mind stream of the meditator with blessings and spiritual powers. As this light enters the meditator-as-deity, gross and subtle obscurations and all kinds of habitual instincts and impurities are expelled. The meditator instantly accumulates the two types of merit and the four empowerments. The mantra's power and the radiating and absorbing light enable the meditator to fully receive all blessings and empowerments. In some generation stage practices, the practitioner receives the four states of vidyadharahood simultaneously with the four empowerments.

Light radiates once again and penetrates the three realms of cyclic existence, penetrating each and every sentient being in all of the six realms, immediately purifying them of all deluded states, afflictions, obscurations and suffering, even suffering that has not yet ripened. The body, speech and mind of all sentient beings become the three states of vajra body, speech and mind, and all sentient beings are liberated in their true, buddha nature. By reciting the mantra in this way, one effects "trin ley"(Tib. *'phrin las*), "concerned activity" for the sake of others. This is the mantra which is likened to a king's messenger.

The fourth type of mantra, which is likened to a bee's hive, is used when many practitioners gather to perform a "drub chen" (Tib. *grub chen*), a "great accomplishment," which may last many days, weeks or months. The "bee's hive" mantra is applied in this context in the following way: from the mantra light radiates boundlessly, pervading every direction, transforming the entire external world into clear light. All ordinary material elements are cleansed and transformed. All appearances are clear light, and the world appears as a pure land. A great celestial palace appears at the center of this purified environment, and all sentient beings appear as deities. All discursive thoughts and delusions have been cleansed. All sounds are the mantra, and all sentient beings reciting the mantra together make a sound like the buzz and vibration of a beehive. The mind assumes a state which recollects and delights in bliss and clarity. This mind is beyond discursive and neurotic thought patterns, beyond clinging to subject and object. You recite the mantra in this state of original wisdom, bringing ultimate benefit to yourself and others in a non-dual way.

This completes the teaching on the four types of mantra recitation. Of course, you will not perform these four simultaneously. Each sadhana will employ one of these four only.

The Manner of Reciting Mantras

The fifth section of the yoga of speech discusses the manner in which recitation is made. When one recites a mantra, it is extremely important to maintain single-pointed concentration (Skt. *samadhi*) upon the three yogas of body, speech and mind. We have already covered the teachings on the yoga of body, wherein you visualize yourself as the deity and maintain awareness of the three pith aspects of that visualization. After you gain control of the deity visualization, your mind then focuses on the mantric syllables. Your mind should be in a state of pure awareness as it moves with the mantra's syllables. It is very important to settle your mind into concentration on the syllables, the sound of the mantra, and the other elements of practice. Dismiss discursive thoughts, concentrate on the visualization, and rigpa—pure awareness—will arise.

The teachings say to abandon mental wandering when reciting mantras. Yet some teachers recite mantras—you can see their lips moving and hear the sounds—even while they are engaged in conversation or while going here and there. These teachers already control "dagba rabjam" (Tib. *dag pa rab 'byams*), "all-pervasive pure perception." Every aspect of their awareness is completely purified. Although you may think they see you as a disciple, in fact they see you as a mantric syllable or a mantra, like the Vajra Guru mantra. These beings know your speech as mantra and know that your mind and theirs are inseparable in the expanse of primordial wisdom. They are entirely established in this space of pure awareness and never leave it. Whether in conversation, eating or reciting mantra, it is all the same. Once you achieve this level, you will not need to be concerned with practice because practice becomes effortless. At this level, the generation stage and completion stage are complete; one experiences only the result and need make no effort to cause the arising of wisdom. When your mind wanders, you must move it back to the process of training. You train by maintaining this flow of awareness to the best of your ability. Everything you do in your practice is training, until you obtain the result that makes effort unnecessary.

If the mind wanders even the tiniest bit when you are reciting the mantra, your practice will accomplish nothing. Even though you are in a state of fully accomplished deity yoga and have generated the deity, the mandala and every aspect of the sadhana, your efforts will be wasted. It does not matter what kind of practice or deity you are trying to accomplish; you will not have any attainment or gain any powers. The obscurations of your speech might diminish from reciting the mantra in this fashion, but you will certainly not accomplish the results you are seeking through the sadhana.

A quote from Guru Rinpoche says, "A person who experiences mental wandering while performing vajra recitation will never achieve any result, even from reciting the mantra for an eon of time."

Of course, this is not surprising. If, while speaking to someone, you fail to look them in the face and instead allow your vision to wander everywhere else, you cannot establish the mental, visual or personal contact that would make your conversation a meaningful exchange. Similarly, if you recite mantra with a wandering mind, you cannot comprehend the substance of the mantra. So how can you expect to achieve results? You are just playing a game.

Next, the text discusses the counting of mantras with a mala. Another quote from the second Buddha, Padmasambhava, says: "The best type of mala to use to increase the number of recitations is a mala made from some type of precious jewel (Tib. *rin po che*). A mediocre type of mala is made from the seed of a tree or fruit, and inferior type of mala is made from wood, earth, stone or medicine."

A mala made from seashells, earth, wood or seeds from trees or fruit is meant to be used to accomplish peaceful sadhanas and peaceful action. A mala made from gold will accomplish expansive karmas. A red coral mala is best for accomplishing powerful sadhanas. A steel or turquoise mala is good for wrathful activity. A mala made from *dzi* or other precious stones can be used to accomplish any of the karmic activities you are doing.

A mala made from apricot stones will accomplish expansive activity. A mala made from "lot ton" (a tiny, round black seed within a fruit) accomplishes powerful activity. A mala made from raksha beads accomplishes wrathful practices. A mala made from bodhi seeds accomplishes all dharmas. Malas of bodhi tree wood accomplish peaceful karmas. A mala of mulberry beads accomplishes powerful karmas. Malas of mahogany wood accomplish wrathful practices. Malas made of ivory, especially from an elephant's tusk, will accomplish all concerned activity.

Beads made of stone are good for expansive practice. Beads made of medicine are good for wrathful practice. Malas with many different types of jewels are good for any practice. However, I suggest that you not attempt to create a mala with a lot of different beads on it because, unless you know which combinations are effective, you may cause a non-positive result.

Next, the text mentions the different kinds of benefits that are derived from using different types of malas.

An iron or steel mala multiplies the virtue that is accumulated with each recitation in a general way. A copper mala multiplies each recitation four times. A raksha mala multiplies each recitation by 20 million, and a pearl mala by 100 million. A silver mala multiplies by 100,000 and a ruby mala by 100 million. A bodhi seed mala manifests limitless benefits for any form of practice, be it peaceful, expansive, powerful or wrathful.

You should all know the mala's meaning and the best way to string it. String your mala using three, five or nine strings, and no other number. Three strings symbolize the three kayas, five strings symbolize the five buddhas, and the nine strings symbolize the nine vehicles.

The main guru bead may be composed of three beads, symbolizing the three vajra states of being, the three kayas. The smallest bead on the outside should be blue, perhaps made of lapis. The color blue symbolizes the unchanging mind of ultimate truth. The bead in the middle should be red, to symbolize vajra speech, and the innermost bead should be white, to symbolize the vajra body.

Your mala must be blessed by a lama, and you should constantly bless your mala yourself by imbuing it with energy. You must put energy into your mala before counting recitations with it, to produce real benefit.

You should clean your mouth and hand, and then your mala, before using it. You may also scent it with sandalwood oil.

Next, generate yourself as the deity, place the mala in your left hand and arrange the beads with the guru bead placed vertically in the center. Recite the mantra that transforms all dharmas into the awareness of their true nature: OM SWABAVA SHUDDO SARVA DHARMA SWABAVA SHUDDO HAM. This mantra cleanses and transforms impure perceptions into the awareness of emptiness.

From emptiness, the guru bead appears as the central deity in the mandala, and the other beads appear as the members of the entourage. This part of the practice is the meditation upon the samayasattva. Next, invoke the jnanasattva. Invite the primordial wisdom beings to come forth, hooking them so that they dissolve into the samayasattva, just as you would in a sadhana. Invite the wisdom beings to come from their pure lands into the space in front of you. They then dissolve into your mala and remain firm there. Thus, every part of your mala is the entire mandala. This includes the central deity, entourage, lotus seats, ornaments, hand emblems, colors, etc. Blessing your mala in this way multiplies each syllable of whatever mantra you then recite 100,000 times, besides causing good karmic results. Therefore, it is extremely important to do this.

Your mala represents not only the form of the deity but the speech of the deity as well. For example, if you recite the One-Hundred-Syllable mantra, the guru bead represents the syllable OM and the other beads represent the remaining syllables.

Guru Padmasambhava said, "Whenever you recite peaceful mantras, use the tip of your thumb to count the mala. When reciting expansive mantras, use the third finger. Use the ring finger and thumb when reciting powerful mantras, and use the little finger when reciting wrathful mantras." Use only your left hand to count mantras. The right hand is but rarely used; for instance, in some wrathful practices. Some books teach the use of both hands, but do not use the right hand only.

Whatever kind of practice you are doing, whether peaceful, wrathful, powerful or expansive, always be aware that the thumb is a vajra hook which hooks spiritual powers, deities and other blessings. It is also easy to move the beads with your thumb.

The text does not elaborate, but there are some extensive teachings on how to move the beads on the malas when performing certain practices. In some wrathful practices, you jerk the beads with both hands and so forth.

The following teachings, which explain how to care for your mala when you are not using it, come straight from the mouth of Guru Padmasambhava. If your mala has been repeatedly blessed by great lamas, by your own teacher and by yourself as part of your deity practice, it should accompany you like your shadow. You keep the root samaya of the vajra mala by never letting it leave your body.

Many branch words of honor relate to the proper care and use of the mala, but only a few are mentioned here. Never let it leave the heat of your body. Never show your secret vajra mala to another person. Never put your mala in other people's hands. Do not pass it around or entrust it to the care of others. And never let your mala pass into the hands of a person who has broken his or her vows, or whose spiritual beliefs are sharply different from your own.

Hold your mala only when doing mantra recitation. Do not play or fumble with it nervously at other times. Do not perform divinations on your mala or tally sums on it.

Keep your mala private and have a humble attitude towards it. Do not flash it around for others to notice. Never put it in a low place, and certainly never on the ground. Do not put beads on your mala that have no meaning and do not put beads on it for adornment's sake. If you keep these words of honor concerning your mala, you will achieve whatever you seek to accomplish.

The teaching that was just given was for a mala that has been blessed many times. On the other hand, if you have an ordinary mala, one that has not been blessed and does not mean very much to you, you can play around with it however you like.

It is very important to protect your mala from contamination by non-virtuous persons. Even a special mala of bodhi seed or gold can cease to be of benefit to anyone. If it contacts the hands of a person who has committed any of the five heinous crimes, you will fail in whatever you try to accomplish. A mala that contacts the hands of a butcher, or someone who broke a vajra vow, or someone who killed another human being, or of a thief or a robber, will be of no benefit to you.

Malas that are acquired from an improper source, or which are incomplete or damaged in certain ways should not be used. A mala that has been blessed and offered to a deity at some time, perhaps to be worn as an ornament, may never be converted to personal use. It would be very negative to think, "Now that it has been blessed, I will take it and use it." Of course, it would be extremely negative to steal and resell such a mala. A mala with more or less than 108 beads is not fit to be used. A mala that has been burned, walked over by an animal, or nibbled at by a mouse is no good. If

your mala has any of these problems, the value of your vajra recitation will be impaired. You should get rid of the mala because it is
useless.

These teachings were not given by the Precious Guru so that
you would become so attached to your mala that you would not
show it to others. These teachings were given because, as a
Vajrayana practitioner, you need a consecrated mala to perform
vajra recitations. The mala is viewed as the root deity with the entire assembly and mandala. As a Vajrayana practitioner, you take
the mala as your source of refuge and thus achieve spiritual powers and blessings on an extraordinary, supreme level and not merely
on an ordinary level. Therefore, you are instructed to rely on your
mala in these ways.

The next section concerns the proper approach to mantra recitation. Do not recite a mantra so swiftly that the syllables run together and lose their individual sense; do not recite it too slowly
either. Recite at a moderate speed, very cleanly and purely, in a
manner that allows you to hear yourself pronounce each syllable.
Do not put in extra syllables and sounds, and do not omit any. Do
not recite the mantra too loudly or too softly. Do not speak to others while reciting mantra. Do not mix mantra by going back and
forth between different mantras. Do not recite mantras with a wandering mind.

If, while reciting a mantra, you must speak a few words to someone, then you must move back four beads for each word you speak.
So, if you have a long conversation, you will be going backwards
for quite some time. If you cough when reciting a mantra, go back
five beads. If you yawn, go back three. If you sneeze, go back ten.
If you spit, go back one. Sometimes people will recite a mantra but
their tongues and lips are barely moving. This is not a proper way
to recite. Obviously, it is best not to do any of these things when
you recite mantras.

It is very good to hold a "gentle vase" of air while reciting mantras. To do this, bring the vital air down into your navel area and
retain it there. Focus your mind on the form and sound of the syllables. This practice will obstruct all discursive thoughts. If you
have not yet received the teachings on *lung* or "vital air," wait
until you receive them before attempting this.

Some vajra recitations are called "mental recitations," because no sound is made during recitation. The mind simply focuses on the syllables.

The commentary that accompanies your particular sadhana will explicitly tell you how to recite the particular mantra in your sadhana. Just follow the instructions of your sadhana. You should recite mantras clearly and evenly, neither too loudly nor too softly, neither too quickly nor too slowly. You should recite them in such a way that you can hear the sound of your own voice but also move along at a fairly rapid pace. Since you are beginners, this is the best way to get the most blessings and results.

It is good to know about holding the vital air and doing mental recitation, but you need not concern yourself with these techniques just now. If you focus on mental recitation now, you will not learn how to perform audible recitation. Furthermore, since our minds are constantly wandering, how can you expect your mental recitation to be effective?

Mantras are recited to utilize sound, form and the power of speech to bring the mind under control. A wandering mind, out of control, prevents one from remaining in a state of perfect peace and frustrates all efforts to direct the mind. Mantra recitation helps regain the noble qualities of mind. Practice must be sincere, however. There are many meditators who close their mouths and move the beads around their malas, supposedly doing mental recitation; but, if you ask them to pronounce the syllables of the mantra they are mentally reciting, they are unable to do so. On the other hand, some Western students say, "I don't like to chant mantras. I'm just going to meditate with my mind." But they cannot prevent their minds from wandering for more than one second. So how are they going to meditate with their minds? They sit, looking like meditators, but they are really just passing a few moments in a nihilistic or eternalistic state. At this stage, it is very difficult for you to practice non-conceptual meditation and achieve valid results. Therefore, mantra recitation is extremely important.

Number of Recitations

The sixth section of the yoga of speech concerns measuring the accumulation of mantra recitations. How do you know when you have recited enough of a particular mantra? Generally speaking, you should count a mantra until you achieve some common spiritual power and ideally until you achieve the supreme spiritual attainment. Wouldn't that be the best way?

After all, if you are really hungry, don't you eat until you are satisfied? Similarly, if you plan a trip to San Francisco, you want to travel until you arrive at your destination. You would not travel halfway and be satisfied with that, would you? In the same way, when you recite a mantra, you have a specific goal in mind: to gain the supreme spiritual attainment—buddhahood. Wouldn't it be wise to keep on reciting the mantra until you have achieved your goal, or at least until you achieve some perceptible improvement?

From a scholarly viewpoint and for the purpose of ordinary discussion, you should recite the mantra 100,000 times for each syllable of the essence mantra before saying that you have accomplished your particular deity. That would be the minimum number. For example, Vajrasattva's mantra has one hundred syllables in it. Therefore, if you are accomplishing the Vajrasattva practice, you must recite this mantra 100x100,000 times, or 10 million times.

This is the number of mantra recitations to recite for the main deity in the mandala. An extensive sadhana will also prescribe mantras for the subsidiary deities in the mandala. If you do 100,000 recitations of the mantra of the main deity in the mandala, then 10,000 recitations of the mantras of the other deities are done as well. If you do 10,000 recitations of the main deity's mantra, then do 1,000 of the other deities' mantras.

It is traditional to make up for all the mistakes you inevitably make when doing your 100,000 recitations by reciting an additional 10,000 mantras at the end. If you have recited only 10,000 of the main deity's mantra, then recite 1,000 extra. If you recite one hundred mantras, then do ten extra. You should always do this. This concludes the teaching on vajra recitation.

Activity Upon Completion

The seventh division of the yoga of speech is the conclusion. When you finish reciting the mantra of your particular sadhana, three things should immediately follow: the first is making offerings and rendering praise; the second is receiving the "spiritual attainment" (Tib. *dngos grub*, pronounced "ngu drup"); the third is asking for forbearance. If it is time to conclude a session, always do these things so that your practice will be properly concluded. The teachings on offerings and praise were taught earlier, so review them.

As the fruit of completing the mantra recitation, the purpose of your practice and whatever you wish for will be accomplished. This is the meaning of the term "receiving spiritual attainment." Usually the phrase is used to describe the process of receiving ordinary spiritual attainments. Actually, there are two kinds of spiritual attainments: ordinary and supreme. There are eight ordinary spiritual attainments and eight obstacles to achieving those eight. More extensive sadhanas have the meditator receive the eight spiritual powers but shorter sadhanas generally will not. Some sadhanas omit entirely any reference to receiving spiritual attainment.

You might then wonder whether you will receive the attainment if it is not specifically part of your practice, but you need not worry about this. Performing any generation stage practice enables you to receive spiritual attainment. Whether it is mentioned in your sadhana or not, the whole point of the generation stage practice, from beginning to end, is to generate and receive spiritual attainment. After performing the vajra recitation, a practitioner will receive spiritual attainment regardless of which deity has been relied upon in practice.

Receiving the spiritual attainment protects you from the eight fears and pacifies all non-conducive conditions that arise in meditation practice. It facilitates the emergence of conducive circumstances. During this present life and in future lifetimes, it gives you the power to overcome poisonous tendencies in yourself and in others, like wrong view and doubt. One who has attained this power can completely exorcise negativities in the minds of others by enacting the four types of miraculous activities: peace, expanse, power and especially wrath, an expression of compassionate power.

When you generate yourself as the main deity, you receive the spiritual attainments that enable you to accomplish any purpose that you might conceive. To "generate yourself as a deity" means to embody the three vajra states of being: the unchanging body, the unobstructed speech and the unmoving mind. This state of being is completely free of the ordinary ego's body, speech and mind, which are conditioned by obscurations and habitual instincts.

By assuming identity with the deity, you open yourself to receive the excellent blessing that transmutes these three entrances into the indestructible three vajras.

Pray to receive the supreme spiritual attainment, the rainbow light body that Guru Padmasambhava accomplished. This is the mahamudra, the state in which bliss and emptiness are indivisible. Desiring to achieve this perfect form, the ultimate form of being, pray that this supreme attainment, the Great Seal, may be bestowed upon you.

There are two kinds of rainbow light bodies. The first, called the "great rainbow light body," was achieved by Guru Padmasambhava when he passed from this world. His physical form completely dissolved into light molecules, leaving no trace behind, while his mind, of course, remained in its original state of primordial awareness. The second type of rainbow light body, called simply the "rainbow light body," is achieved by dissolving the body entirely into light, leaving only hair and fingernails. Many practitioners attained the rainbow light body before the Communist Chinese takeover of Tibet.

All that has been discussed until now—generating the pure awareness of perfect stability and clarity of the visualization, hearing all sounds as mantra, and perceiving the mind as pure awareness and form as the illusory nature—are the generation stage Vajrayana methods. The completion stage aspect of the practice is effected by applying these methods with full understanding of their empty nature. Through the method, great bliss is achieved, and through awareness of the empty nature of that bliss, great wisdom is achieved. Mahamudra realization, the supreme spiritual attainment, is direct realization of the indivisibility of bliss and emptiness. When this attainment is achieved, the rainbow light body is achieved. This is achieving the state of Buddha Vajradhara.

With single-pointed mind and fervent devotion, pray to receive the supreme realization. Next, visualize that from the entire assembly of deities which you have been visualizing, from their three centers—the crown, throat and heart—light radiates forth: white light from their crowns, red light from their throats and blue light from their hearts. As this light radiates and dissolves into your three centers, feel certain that all of the supreme spiritual attainments that we have been speaking of dissolve into you. The common spiritual attainments come of themselves, giving you the power to do whatever you desire.

The third thing that is done following mantra recitation is to beseech the deity for forbearance. You should unveil, with a deep sense of remorse, all the mistakes and failings that have occurred during your sadhana. Confess all faults, such as performing recitation and visualization carelessly, succumbing to delusion, failing to maintain proper view, meditation and conduct, deviating from the true meaning of the practice out of confusion, and so forth. Single-pointed, clear visualization of the deity is the most important thing to accomplish in the generation stage practice. If you have failed to actualize the three pith elements of proper visualization, of which we have spoken—clear, focused concentration upon the deity's form, stable vajra pride, and pure recollection of the meaning of the deity's characteristics—confess this carelessness at this point in the practice. Recite the One-Hundred-Syllable mantra to instantly purify these faults. You do not need to perform a separate Vajrasattva practice and generate the entire visualization; purification occurs instantly.

You should also confess and purify the mistakes you made during mantra recitation by omitting or inserting words, as well as any faults accrued concerning the offering materials. For example, you might confess the fact that you were poor and were unable to offer proper materials, or that you were too lazy to arrange the offerings properly. Mostly, you should confess your ignorance of the proper ways to practice, your lack of faith, and your avarice. Then, recite the verses which beseech forbearance and reflect on their meaning.

CHAPTER VI

The Actual Practice:
The Yoga of Meditative Equipoise
Part III

The Yoga of Clear Light

The body and speech yogas are now complete. Now begins the third division, the mind yoga of clear light, which is discussed in terms of the object of purification, the practice of purification, and the result.

The object to be purified by the mind yoga of clear light is one's own condition. From the time of conception in the womb through birth, childhood, adulthood and old age, one works, marries and pushes forward, moving toward death. The object of purification is the entire stream of samsaric events, including your future death, bardo experience and rebirth. The entire cycle of successive lives is purified by performing the mind yoga of clear light.

Dissolve your visualization beginning with the outer perimeter of the pure land, the pure perception of the ordinary universe. The outer pure land gradually dissolves into the wheel of protection. Stage by stage, everything dissolves inward until eventually you come to the very heart of the central deity where you dissolve the mantric syllables into the seed syllable, which then dissolves into emptiness.

This dissolution practice purifies the stages of dissolution that occur at the time of death. The first stage begins a chain reaction of the outer moving inwardly, which further moves into the moment of death itself. At death the clear light arises, the Dharmakaya, the true, ultimate state of being which all beings reach at the moment of death after all the elements of life have dissolved. Dissolving the visualization in this way brings one to this moment of clear light.

Whether death occurs quickly or slowly, as the dying process continues, the experiences of the sense fields relating to sense perceptions, and the subject relating with the objects, are cut off one by one. Eventually, perception through the sense fields ceases and a state of complete emptiness occurs. Immediately thereafter, a very wondrous sensation occurs, like an experience of awakening. As you dissolve the various stages of the visualization, imagine that this wondrous sensation occurs.

This process is identical to that which occurs the moment you fall asleep. You do not just close your eyes and fall asleep immediately. Rather, your outer experiences dissolve slowly into inner experiences, and then you fall asleep. At this moment, the clear light arises, which is the true, ultimate state of being. This state lasts for a certain period of time, and immediately thereafter dreams begin. This same process occurs at death. The duration of the clear light experience at the time of death varies, depending on individual karma and the amount of meditation practice a person has done. As soon as the clear light passes, the images and phenomena of the Bardo of Intrinsic Reality begin.

This Dharmakaya experience also arises the moment one thought stops and just before the next thought begins. That split second holds the same experience of clear light that occurs at death and between the waking and sleeping states. Simply sitting with your mouth hanging open will not lead you to the clear light experience. The practice which purifies the object is the entire practice as it has been taught from the beginning up until now, including all the stages of visualization and particularly the generation of the three meditative absorptions and visualizations of the meditational being and the seed syllable.

To complete the sadhana, it is necessary to train in the stages of dissolution. Dissolution begins when your awareness of the most external aspects of the mandala—the external world as pure land with all animate beings—dissolves into light and into the wheel of protection. The wheel of protection then dissolves into the lowest of the four elements that are visualized heaped upon each other: earth, water, fire and air. Each of the elements then dissolves into light, and the light is absorbed into the element above it until all are dissolved. The elements dissolve into the internal wheel of protection, which dissolves into the charnel ground, which dissolves into the celestial mansion, which dissolves into the assembly of deities, which dissolves into the central deity and consort. The consort dissolves into the central deity, who then dissolves into the wisdom being in his heart. The wisdom being dissolves into the seed syllable (the absorption being) in his heart, and then the seed syllable dissolves, from the bottom upward, until everything has been completely dissolved into emptiness.

At this point, nothing is left to visualize. Experience this state of mind which is beyond activity, free of contrivance. Rest in this perfect state of emptiness, without thought, as long as you can. This state of equipoise purifies the extreme of eternalism.

After dissolving the visualization and reaching the clear light meditation, you arise again as the deity, complete with mandala. In this way, you purify the Sipa (Tib. *srid pa*) Bardo, the Bardo of Existence.

When you first stir from non-conceptual meditation, you recite the deity's root mantra and immediately arise as the perfect form of the central deity, like a fish jumping out of water. You are surrounded by the entire mandala and the assembly of deities. The visualization appears as it was before the dissolution. Unite your awareness with this mandala as unwaveringly as a flowing river, seeing all beings as the deity, hearing all sounds as the mantra, and keeping your mind and the mind of all beings always in a state of pure awareness. This practice of reawakening as the deity, complete with mandala, purifies the extreme of nihilism.

The result of the purification process is achieving the Nirmanakaya, the manifestation being of the Buddha, which is an expression of the concerned activity of the Dharmakaya. This form is expressed as both the Sambhogakaya (illusory form) and Nirmanakaya (manifestation form). Arising as the deity is the arising of primordial wisdom expressed by way of Sambhogakaya and Nirmanakaya.

Everything that you have learned thus far regarding the generation stage practice—meaning, practice and result—has been sealed with the awareness of the empty nature. This expresses the indivisibility of appearance and emptiness, generation stage and completion stages. After the various stages of the visualization have been completely developed, they are dissolved into clear light. Then, from this clear light, the illusory form of the deity arises. These practices eliminate the two extreme views of eternalism and nihilism.

CHAPTER VII

The Actual Practice:
The Yoga of Arising from Equipoise

After dissolving all appearances into the clear light and remaining in non-conceptual meditation for as long as you are able, the yoga of the post-meditational experience begins the moment the play of conceptual, discursive mind begins. At this point you instantaneously re-arise as the illusory form of the deity complete with entourage, celestial palace and all the elaborations. The entire visualization that you had previously generated re-arises instantaneously. Thereafter, in your post-meditational experience, you will experience all appearances as the deity, hear the nature of all sounds as mantras, and recognize the nature of thought formation to be pure awareness. You will maintain the play of deity, mantra and primordial wisdom awareness in your daily life experience. When you are going here and there, sitting and moving, you will see all activity as the mudra of the deity. When you are eating and drinking, you will offer these substances as an inner fire offering as they are consumed by the body. Any of the desirable objects that you utilize become the play of the three awarenesses: the empty nature of subject, object and activity. This is called carrying the post-meditational experience as the path.

One should train diligently in the practice of dissolving appearances into the clear light and then re-emerging. This can be done at the time of sleep. When you fall asleep, this is the dissolution and, as the dream bardo arises, this is the re-emergence. Or, as you wake up from sleep, this is the re-emergence. You should train in this yoga of post-meditational experience as diligently as possible.

Now here there may be a question: "Is it only myself I am experiencing as the deity, hearing all sounds as mantras and recognizing all thought to be wisdom?" This experience is non-dual; there is no distinction between yourself and all phenomena, all experience. The experience of the primordial wisdom nature is completely free of all delusion. Don't think that the five poisons are present in that state.

CHAPTER VIII

The Completion

The third division of this teaching is the completion. We have completed the preliminaries and the actual practice; the completion
involves dedication of merit, closing prayers and prayers for good
fortune and for all to be auspicious.

For dedication of merit, recall the bodhicitta attitude that you
generated at the very beginning of the practice. Recall that the reason you have committed yourself to perform this profound yoga
is to liberate all sentient beings from their suffering and establish
them in the state of permanent bliss and happiness. It is for this
reason that you have been performing the meditation of the generation and, later, the completion stage yogas. At this point, as your
practice concludes, it is extremely important to dedicate the root
of your virtue and merit for the sake of all these beings just as you
promised to do. In this way, your practice is sealed.

No matter how big or small, one must never forget to dedicate one's merit and virtue to the unsurpassed awakening of all parent sentient beings. As it is said in the *Lodroe Gyatso Shupai Sutra* (*Blo gros rgya mtsos shus pa'i mdo*), just as one drop of water when put in the ocean will remain as long as the ocean remains and will not become exhausted until the ocean is dry, if one dedicates the root of one's virtue and merit with the bodhicitta attitude, it will never be exhausted until the awakening of all beings is achieved. Otherwise, if you forget to dedicate your virtue and merit, then because of the intensity of the poisons, such as anger and hatred, one moment of anger will destroy any virtuous accumulations. Virtue and merit that has not been dedicated is like dry grass and one moment of anger is like fire put to the grass, consuming it instantly. But if the virtue has already been dedicated it can never be destroyed, because it has joined the vast ocean of the enlightened mind of all the buddhas. Therefore, always dedicate your merit in this manner.

The supreme way to dedicate your merit is to realize the empty nature of subject, object and activity, and to remain in the equipoise. If one is not able to do this, if one does not have the potential, one should consider that "just as all the buddhas and bodhisattvas of the past have generated the bodhicitta and dedicated their virtue and merit with prayers, so too do I make a similar dedication," and recite whatever verses are found in the sadhana practice.

The second part of the conclusion consists of prayers that are made immediately after dedication. These prayers should be made, as Guru Rinpoche said, with faith and compassion, for the purpose of the awakening and liberation of all other parent sentient beings. One should make pure, heartfelt prayers and dedications for their welfare with the very broad bodhicitta motivation that one has given rise to earlier in the practice. Whatever heartfelt prayers one may wish to make can be made at this time. One should recite the verses in the sadhana and can include any other prayers that are commonly made at this time.

Finally, the third part of the conclusion is the prayer for all to be auspicious. At this time, visualize that in the space in front are the Three Root deities, the Three Jewels, and all of the assemblies of meditational deities. Consider that they are truly present. They all sing the song for auspicious good fortune and a gentle rainfall of flowers begins falling from all directions. Consider that the flowers and the sound of the prayers for good fortune are all-pervasive and vast, like massing cloud formations. Repeat the verses in your sadhana practice for all to be auspicious, and you may throw some flower petals or rice into the space in front of you. Know that, without failure, the prayer will be answered; good fortune and auspicious circumstances will prevail.

Within the generation stage practice, just as in the completion stage, one must maintain the view, meditation and conduct. Briefly, the view is established by developing an understanding of the nature of the mind which is void of substance, color, shape or any other characteristic. Once you understand that this mind lacks true, independent, inherent existence, you can clear away the eternalistic delusion that believes "something exists." Yet, at the same time, you should understand the mind to be perfectly pure and unobstructed by its very nature—a ceaseless state of pure awareness. This understanding counters the nihilistic tendency to believe that mind must be negated. Thus the view, properly established, eliminates the four extreme views: eternalism, nihilism, neither eternalism nor nihilism, and both eternalism and nihilism.

The mind is beyond expression, thought and conceptualization, because it is empty. Yet, there is phenomena and appearance. The objects that you cling to in this waking reality are dreamlike, but if you do not inquire into the nature of this dream, you remain attracted as though there were really something here. Upon examination, you find that these objects have no true existence at all and are just like space. A practitioner who understands that phenomena lack inherent existence and resemble space should then examine himself or herself to discover whether he or she possesses an individual self. Then it will be discovered that there is no truly existing examiner either.

The view is called "the view of self-arisen primordial wisdom," because it is the realization that appearance and pure awareness are naked and not distinct from one's own true nature. Appearance and pure awareness are simply self-born. They arise from self and from no other source. This is the view.

True meditation is remaining in the state of mind which is neither tight nor loose. Nothing needs to be cleared away from that mind and nothing needs to be placed there. The meditative state of mind is free from activity and never wavers from its original nature. It just rests naturally; it is perfectly clear, naked and unchanging. It is the indivisibility of mental quiescence (Tib. *gzhi gnas*, Skt. *śamatha*) and panoramic awareness (Tib. *lhag mthong*, Skt. *vipaśyanā*). Mind in its natural state is true meditation.

Conduct requires that one remain ever united with, and never be separate from, the view and meditation—never! This is your conduct. Be very conscientious concerning all aspects of conduct, and carry the spontaneously born primordial wisdom and great bliss as your activity on the path.

By practicing the sadhana, you achieve proper view, meditation and conduct. Additionally, you obtain realization of the true nature of reality as it is, directly perceived on the conventional plane. There is nothing to abandon or achieve. The realization and perception of the ultimate true state of beings, the Dharmakaya, is the result.

To conclude this teaching it is important to realize here, and it has already been said, that you have in no way created a result or caused a result to occur. The result is the original cause. The practice has simply been performed to remove the clouds from the sun, to remove obscurations so that the original nature is unveiled and directly perceived. The sun in never stained by the clouds. It always remains pure. The nature, the result, has been pure from the original beginning, and the moment one finally perceives this nature, it is as it always has been.

May virtue and auspiciousness prevail!

Plates

Plate I *OM AH HUM HO Mudra*

Plate II *Casting Out the Torma Mudra*

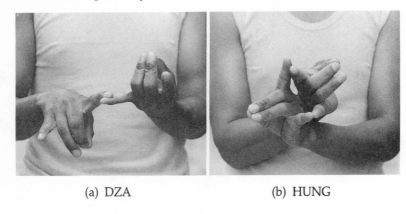

(a) DZA   (b) HUNG

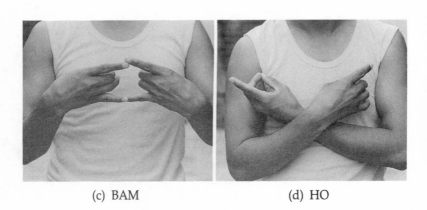

(c) BAM   (d) HO

Plate III   *Attracting the Deity Mudra*

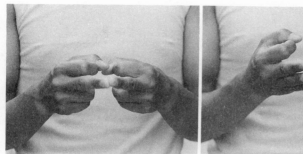

(a) ARGHAM
Water to drink

(b) PADHYAM
Water to bathe

(c) PUSHPE
Flowers

(d) DÜPHE
Incense

Plate IV-1   *Offering Mudras*

(e) ALOKHE
Light

(f) GENDHE
Perfume

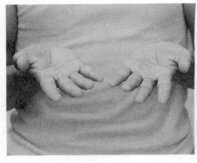
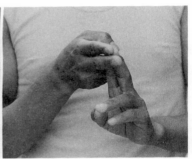

(g) NEVIDHYA
Celestial food

(h) SHABTA
Music

Plate IV-2 *Offering Mudras*

Plate V-1 *Offering Torma (White)*

Plate V-2 *Obstacle Torma (Red)*

(a)

Plate V-3   *(a) Lama, (b)Yidam, (c) Khadroma Tormas*
            (Red with White Trim)

(b)   (c)

Plate VI-1   *Three-dimensional replica of mandala representing peaceful
enlightened activity, built by the monks under the direction of
H.H. Penor Rinpoche at Nyingmapa Monastery in Bylakuppe,
India. Approximately three feet high.*

Plate VI-2   *Close-up of the entrance to the west, charnel ground and vajra fence. Three-dimensional mandala, Nyingmapa Monastery, Bylakuppe, India.*

APPENDIX I

ཨ་ཨཱཿ ཨི་ཨཱི༔ ཨུ་ཨཱུཿ རྀ་རཱྀ༔ ལྀ་ལཱྀ༔ ཨེ་ཨཻ༔ ཨོ་ཨཽ༔ ཨཾ་ཨཿ

AH A̅H, E E̅, OO O̅O, RI R̅I, LI L̅I, AY A̅Y, OH O̅H, AM AH

ཀ་ཁ་ག་ང༔ ཙ་ཚ་ཛ་ཉ༔ ཊ་ཋ་ཌ༔ པ་ཕ་བ་མ༔
ཡ་ར་ལ་ཝ༔ ཤ་ས་ཧ་ཀྵ༔

KA KHA GA GHA NGA, TSA TSHA DSA DZHA NYA, TRA THRA DRA DHRA NRA, TA THA DA DHA NA, PA PHA BA BHA MA, YA RA LA WA, SHA SA HA KYA

APPENDIX II

ༀ	ཨཱཿ	ཧཱུྃ	ཧོ	རཾ	ཡཾ	ཁཾ	ཛ༔	ཧཱུྃ	བཾ	ཧོ
OM	AH	HUNG	HO	RAM	YAM	KHAM	DZA	HUNG	BAM	HO

བྷྲཱུྃ	ཧྲཱི	པཾ	ལཾ	ཏྲཾ	མཾ	བཾ	སཾ	མུཾ	ཏཾ	ཧཾ	ཉྲི
BHRUM	HRI	PAM	LAM	TRAM	MAM	BAM	SUM	MUM	TAM	HAM	NRI

Tibetan calligraphy by Palden Choedak Oshoe

APPENDIX III

Diagrams of Mandalas

Mandala 1

1. God's realm
2. Corner, angle
3. Buttress
4. Inner yard
5. Wall
6. Red verandah
7. Upper ledge
8. Semi-lattice
9. Upper gutters
10. Parapet ornamented with half lotus leaves
11. Passages (four)
12. Doorway
13. Inner doorway
14. Demons lying face downwards
15. Darkness or obscurity
16. Two or more pillars supporting the ledge
17. Decoration of column
18. Inside window opening
19. Window entrance with three arches
20. Blue ledge that supports vajras
21. Lotus above blue ledge
22. Green jeweled casket
23. Latticework
24. Yellow ledge
25. Black space
26. Jeweled gutter
27. Garuda, mythical chief of the feathered race
28. Lotus
29. Dharma wheel
30. Parasol, emblem of royalty
31. Stag and doe
32. Outer yard
33. Lotus enclosure
34. Garland of light
35. Charnel ground
36. Vajra fence
37. Wall of fire

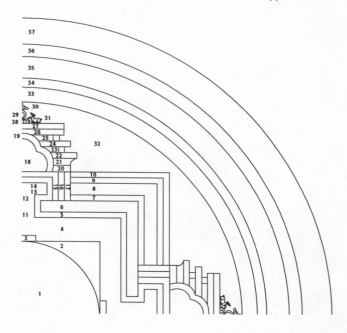

Mandala 1

Mandala 2

Mandala 2

1. God's realm
2. Corner, angle
3. Buttress
4. Inner yard
5. Wall
6. Red verandah
7. Upper ledge
8. Semi-lattice
9. Upper gutters
10. Parapet ornamented with half-lotus leaves
11. Passages (four)
12. Doorway
13. Inner doorway
14. Demons lying face downwards
15. Darkness or obscurity
16. Two or more pillars supporting the ledge
17. Decoration of column
18. Inside window opening
19. Outer yard
20. Ledge
21. Ledge
22. Ledge
23. Ledge
24. Lotus
25. Dharma wheel
26. Parasol, emblem of royalty
27. Stag and doe
28. Window entrance with three arches
29. Lotus enclosure
30. Garland of light
31. Charnel ground
32. Vajra fence
33. Wall of fire

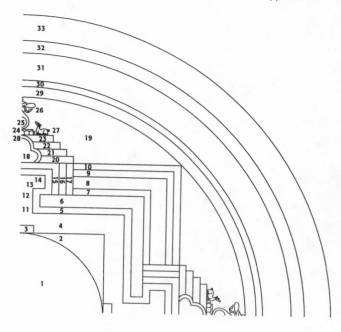